Cliff In His Own Words.

Compiled by Kevin St. John.

Exclusive distributors:
Book Sales Limited,
78 Newman Street, London W1P 3LA.
Quick Fox,
33 West 60th Street, New York,
N.Y. 10023, USA.

Omnibus Press
London/New York/Sydney/Cologne.

Published 1981 by Omnibus Press
(a division of Book Sales Limited).

Book design & origination: Perry Neville.
Design assistant: Gill Lockhart.
Picture research: Perry Neville & Susan Ready.
Original series design: Pearce Marchbank.

Thanks to Peter & Gabrielle Bishop, Nigel, Barney, Miles, and to the Vintage Magazine Shop for supplying pictures and other material.
It has been impossible to identify or trace the photographers responsible for many of the earlier pictures in this book. A special thanks to you all, and apologies for omitting your credits.

ISBN 0-86001-931-4.
UK Order No. OP 41276.

Typeset by G.W. Young Photosetters Limited, Brighton Road, Surbiton, Surrey.
Printed in England by William Clowes (Beccles) Limited, Beccles and London.

The Early Days.

I'd always understood that my grandfather was born in a house on Threadneedle Street in London, but every time I pass through there, all I can see are banks and insurance offices.

Every time I go down there I always wonder where my grandfather's house was. It's all been redeveloped. There's no sign of any houses left at all in that area.

Growing Up In India.

I was born in northern India, in Lucknow, but I spent the first seven years of my life in Howrah, near Calcutta.

My father, whose name was Roger Webb (my real name is Harry Webb), worked for a catering firm called Kellners. They ran the refreshment rooms and restaurant cars of the Bengal Nagpur Railway. I was the eldest of four children. The others are girls – Donella, Joan and Jacqueline.

My earliest memories are mainly very pleasant. I remember the kite-flying of which there is no equal in England. There was even a festival in the spring when the sky would become black with kites. In India kite-flying was taken much more seriously than it is here.

You took your cotton string and rubbed in a mixture of white of egg and finely powdered ground glass, so that it was like a cutting edge. The important thing was to wear leather gloves so that you didn't cut yourself, of course.

The kites were diamond-shaped, in all colours, with the shortest tails. Those are best for flying. The aim was to fly your kite across your opponent's, and then quickly slacken your string so that it cut through his. Then the trick was to play with the wind so that you caught his kite and

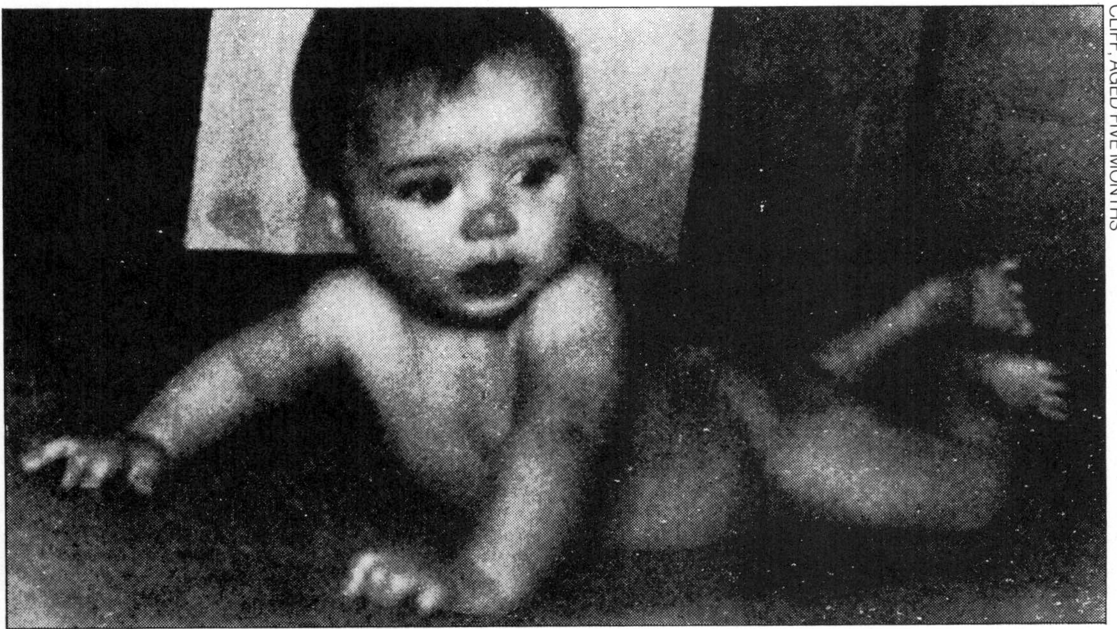

CLIFF, AGED FIVE MONTHS

"tangled" it. If you did that you could claim it as your prize.

It was fascinating. I used to sit for hours watching my Dad flying kites from our roof top.

I remember our long school holidays which we spent with our parents' people, half the period in Lucknow, where my paternal grandfather lived, then going on to my maternal grandmother, at Buxar.

I've never been able to find Buxar on the map. It was just a place where the railway line came to a full stop with a set of bumpers in a field.

It's funny, but very little of Lucknow remains in my memory – just my grandfather's rambling bungalow with a few chickens pecking about outside. However, I can vividly recall Buxar, where we had some wonderful times. Picnics. Fishing with bent pins in the tank there. Fresh cream on our bread and jam for tea.

I went to a church school, St. Thomas's, in Howrah. I remember school lunches, not supplied by the authorities as they are here, but with a servant bringing the food between two plates tied up in a napkin. We sat and ate in a clump of banana trees in the school grounds.

We used to go bee-hunting too, swatting bees with our badminton rackets, killing hundreds of them. It was very dangerous, really, and looking back now I'm horrified that I ever did it. If the bees had swarmed, they could have killed us.

My sister came bee-hunting once, and a bee stung her ear. For many years after that, every time she heard a bee buzzing she'd cover her ears with her hands instinctively.

And there were big monkeys jumping about in the trees – we used to pull faces at them, and they'd chase us.

We also had a green parrot which we kept in a cage. He didn't talk, but he used to whistle. Anyway, one day I put a cloth toy parrot in his cage for him to play with. Well, he started to attack it. And by the time Dad came home, he was dead! He'd tried to fight the toy one, and collapsed with exhaustion.

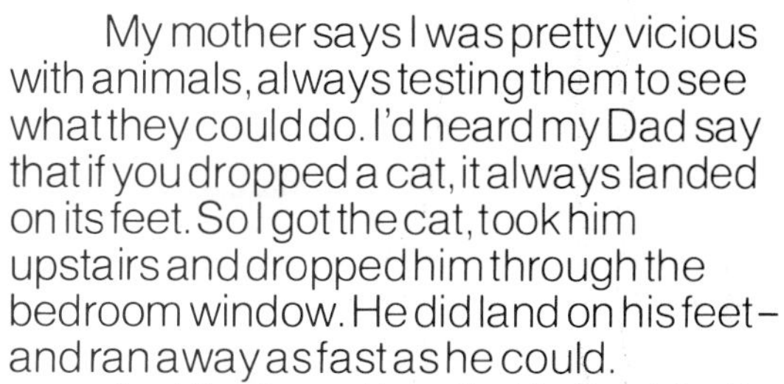

CLIFF, AGED FIFTEEN MONTHS

My mother says I was pretty vicious with animals, always testing them to see what they could do. I'd heard my Dad say that if you dropped a cat, it always landed on its feet. So I got the cat, took him upstairs and dropped him through the bedroom window. He did land on his feet – and ran away as fast as he could.

And I've heard too, that I often tried to eat lizards – yes, it's true! When I was a little kid, I would eat anything I could lay my fingers on. Flowers. Grass. Twigs. Anything. And I've been told that my Dad often used to dive across the floor just in time to stop me popping a lizard in my mouth, because there were lizards everywhere there.

After India's Independence was granted in 1947 we started to talk about going "home" to England. Though both my parents were born and reared in India, we felt very conscious of being foreigners.

There was also the question of our safety. I remember being very excited listening to shots being fired and the sounds of rioting not far from where we lived. I never saw any bodies or anything, but we could hear the guns from our house and for a time the only place I could play was in the backyard.

They never tried to attack our house because a rumour had gone round the area that my Dad had an elephant gun. He'd had one, but by then he'd sold it – but the rumour kept us safe.

Our house was next door to a derelict sewing machine factory, and at one time there was a Mohammedan refugee hiding in there. For two days we threw bread and food over the wall to sustain him, and then after that we smuggled him into our house, and hid him there until it was safe.

Arrival In England.

We eventually arrived in England in September 1948. I can recall being struck by the trees. They appeared to be everywhere, even in the precincts of railway

CLIFF'S FIRST PUBLIC PERFORMANCE WITH THE SCHOOL DRAMATIC SOCIETY

stations, which was something I had not encountered in India.

England was a shining green world daubed with splashes of autumn gold and so clean and neat and well-ordered.

We arrived in England from India with exactly five pounds, and we squeezed in with a grandmother who had eight children in the home.

For seven months after that Dad was unemployed and later on we lived six people to a single room.

Yet we were a happy family, and I remember having more happy and enjoyable times then than any other.

My Grandmother had also come "home" and we lived with her in Surrey, for about a year.

From there we moved to an aunt's place at Waltham Cross, in Hertfordshire, where I attended a primary school for a couple of years, took my 11-plus, failed, and went to Cheshunt Secondary Modern School.

About that time we moved to Cheshunt, and we lived, the six of us in one room – literally. We slept in it, ate in it, it was our kitchen, our toilet.

One day a kind neighbour came in and said, "This is ridiculous." She had a friend on the council who came and saw for herself how we were living. As a result we got a council house, but only after a wait of a further twelve months.

Now the problem was furniture. We had nothing at all. No beds or mattresses – we slept on the floor and there were only boxes to sit on. Later my father made both our armchairs out of packing cases he bought for a shilling each from the firm he worked for.

We became very attached to these chairs and kept them for years after I had

made the grade and we could afford better. They reminded us of our worst days, though I sometimes wonder whether they really *were* our worst days.

I was in the back garden once with my air gun shooting tin cans off the back fence with one of my friends.

He saw a starling sitting on the fence, and said, "Try and shoot that." I just turned and shot with the rifle from the hip – and it dropped down dead.

Great waves of conscience swept over me, and I was suddenly ashamed to realise that I'd actually killed a living creature. It was then I realised how wrong it was to hurt birds and animals – but when you're very young your feelings aren't so finely developed.

I think all little boys are rather callous at times. But after shooting that bird, I know I'd be pretty hopeless if it ever came to being a soldier – I could never bring myself to shoot another human being. Emotionally it's something that I just couldn't do. But it wasn't until that moment when I killed the starling that I realised it.

I suppose that was the moment I started to grow up.

Life was tough but we were by no means unhappy. We were a close-knit family and the sense of security this gave us made up for what we lacked in material things. This is an important factor, I think, in my background.

Another thing, being the oldest child, I was brought into sharing family problems quite early. This developed my sense of responsibility besides giving me the rather nice feeling of being able to co-operate with my parents.

WITH HIS SISTER, JOAN

WITH HIS MOTHER/DEZO HOFFMAN, REX FEATURES

I remember my mother once saying she was afraid there couldn't be any pocket money for me for the next two or three months. I also remember not really minding because I knew the particular reason for what must have been for my parents a very drastic economy.

Both of them went out to work and I had to manage in their absence. At the age of eleven I would get tea for us children after school. This might include making a bottle for my youngest sister who was then a baby. I even changed nappies.

When I have children of my own I shall certainly know how to cope.

My interest in entertaining goes back to about that time. I became involved in the school drama society and usually took lead parts.

The first was a Chinese play called 'The Price Of Perfection.' We also did 'A Christmas Carol' and 'Toad of Toad

Hall' in which I played Ratty. Ratty sings, and after the play quite a number of people said I should sing more.

Three other boys and myself formed a group. We sang at school concerts and I can clearly remember wanting to be a pop singer at fourteen.

The Peter Teague Skiffle Group.

I left school at sixteen and got a job as a clerk in the factory where my father worked.

I had acquired a second-hand guitar, and I joined Peter Teague's Skiffle Group. Skiffle was then the rage, but I couldn't get enthusiastic about that do-it-yourself type music with washboards and home-made basses.

Up until then it was Rosemary Clooney and Teresa Brewer, 'cos that was all there was. And then one night, I don't know if it was on AFN or what, I heard (sings) "Well, Since My Bay-Bee Left Me," and I thought, "Blimey, what's that?" There it was. Immediately that happened there was the Bill Haley thing.

Fats Domino. From then onwards – I'm sorry Rosemary Clooney, as good as she is at her own thing – it was just all over.

I suppose that would be in 1956 and we used to play around locally – clubs and pubs...

I remember one place we just got paid in whatever silver the manager had left at the end of the day. He used to spend most of the evening trying to get paid in paper money and we used to tell everyone to pay him in silver... it wasn't very much, but it was good fun and good experience.

It was there, really, that I met someone called John Foster who said, "Well you know, we could make you a star, kid."

The Drifters.

Terry Smart, the drummer and I broke away to form a group of our own. We called ourselves The Drifters; years later we heard of an American group by this name and changed ours to The Shadows.

In a few months we had got ourselves quite well known locally. I thought we were pretty good so I decided we should come up to London's West End to be discovered.

FIRST PROFESSIONAL ENGAGEMENT, AT BUTLIN'S

AT THE 21'S CLUB

The club where it happened at that time was something called the 2 I's in Soho. It was a real sweathole; small, hot and nasty and if you weren't singing you took turns in the back room working the orange machine.

In fact Bruce and Hank who were later to become my backing group The Shadows, were working the orange machine too, the week I was there. I wonder what their first impressions were, of the greasy-haired slob, singing to the crowd!

Anyway, I sung there for a week. And when I wasn't discovered after that time I packed my guitar and went home, because I really expected to be a star straight away!

Breaking Out In Soho.

I went down to the 2 I's in the hope of finding someone. When I mentioned the fact that I was looking for a lead-guitarist someone down there asked me if I'd heard the thin bloke with glasses playing. I listened and the thin bloke with glasses was immediately asked if he'd like to join us – that's how Hank B. Marvin became a

THE DRIFTERS

Drifter. And don't forget the "B," he's very fussy about it.

However there was a snag. This Geordie wanted his mate along. "Can your mate play?" I asked. "Sure he can," I was told.

Well, it says a lot for the keenness of those two to link up with me. His mate, Bruce Welch, and Hank spent all night practising my numbers and when I heard Bruce the following morning, he was playing good enough to fool me. A full group was being formed.

So, with my two new recruits plus Ian "Sammy" Samwell and Terry Smart, off we went. Now on that tour was another act called "The Most Brothers" and with them was Jet Harris. Jet used to come on stage with us from time to time as extra guitar. But by this time Sammy, who was our bass player, really wanted to come out of the group and concentrate on writing. This gave me the chance of asking Jet to join us, and immediately after that tour, Jet became our bass player.

And then came for me the sad decision. We were getting more profes-sional and my close friend and the group's drummer, Terry Smart, wasn't quite up to it.

Yet Terry was the one who came to see me. He knew the position and his

friendship and feeling for me was such that he told me quite openly that he had always had a hankering to join the Merchant Navy. This I knew to be true for he'd often talked about it. But although he never said it and I didn't refer to it, his decision to join at the time was as much to help me as anything else.

Terry and I are still close friends; nothing that has happened to either of us has changed that. He's one of the few people who knew me as Harry Webb and still treats me just the same as in the old days. He's someone I can relax with completely.

How Harry Webb Became Cliff Richard.

One night a ballroom manager from Derby came in, thought our act pretty good and offered us a one night engagement. We could hardly wait, even though after-

'HUG'

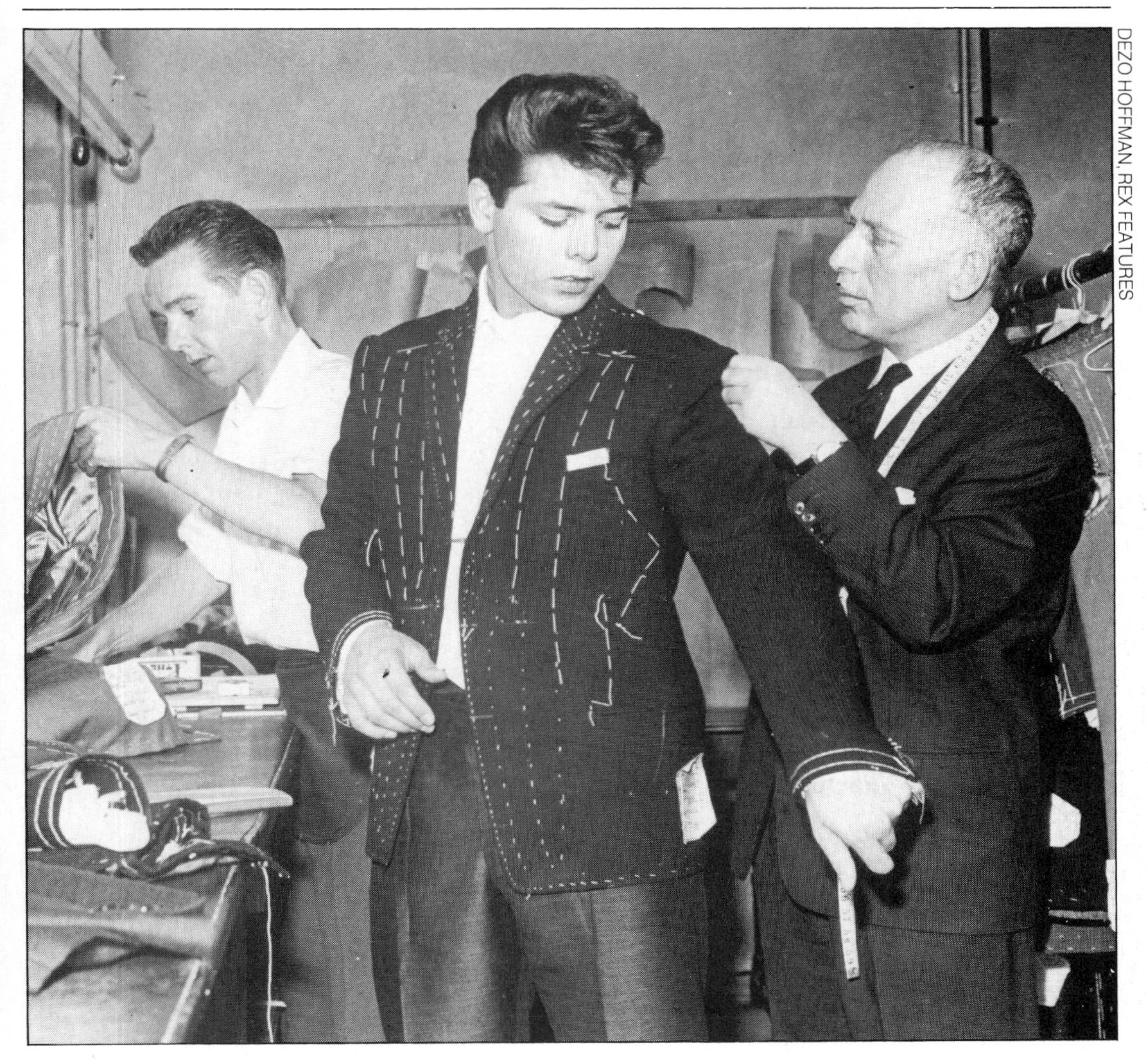

DEZO HOFFMAN, REX FEATURES

wards we realised the money we were getting would barely pay our fare to Derby and back, but it didn't matter – we'd got a real booking – to us, then, it might have been the London Palladium.

"Well, that's fine," said our Derby manager, "But how do I bill you?" "The Drifters," was my reply. "Yes, kid, but you're the singer. What's your name?" "Harry Webb." "Hmph! Harry Webb and The Drifters. Doesn't sound too good to me." It didn't sound too hot to any of us either.

So we went round to the pub and got down to the business of re-christening me. I wasn't too sure that it was necessary – after all we'd always been just The Drifters, why should we now be anything else. But the truth of the matter was that you have to have someone out in front, someone on whom the whole act was pegged. There was Tommy Steele and his Steelmen; later on came Marty Wilde and his Wildcats.

We played around with a lot of names that night and the one I liked best was Richard. I'd always liked the name of Richard. From that point, all it seemed we had to find was a surname to go with it. Then someone said, "Russ Clifford." "Not Russ," I objected. "It's a sort of soft name. How about Cliff Russard?"

It was Johnny Foster, friend and our sort of business manager at the time who slapped his thigh and said, "Just a minute. How about Cliff Richard? And I mean Richard without the 's'. It's a great name

and don't you see, people will always call you Cliff Richards and then we correct them – that way they'll never forget your name."

Moving It.

I went to London for a Carroll Levis talent contest which was being held at the

Gaumont, Shepherd's Bush. It was mid-summer 1958.

I shudder sometimes when I think of our sheer conceit, because when we had a look at the other acts, we went to Levis and told him we'd rather not compete as it

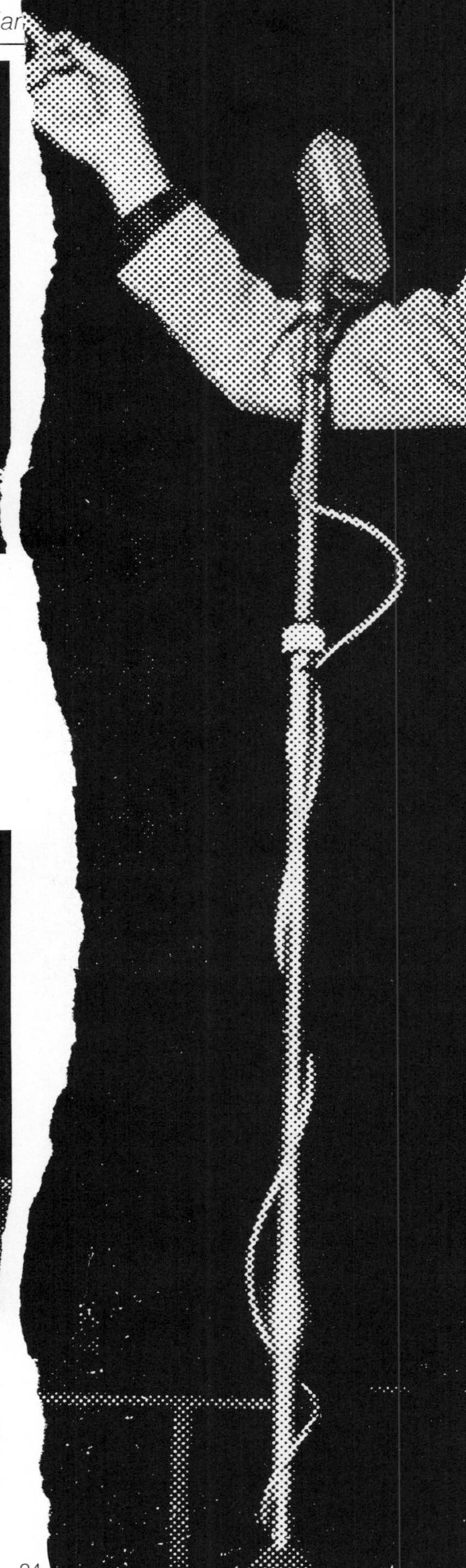

would obviously be a walkover. Instead we suggested we closed the bill.

We got our way and, when we came on, a marvellous reaction from the audience. I'd never heard anything like it.

A month later there was another talent contest at the cinema. We went back on the same conditions, but this time

we invited George Ganjou, the theatrical agent, to sit in the audience. What interested him was not our performance, because he could scarcely hear it, but the response, which was even better than on the previous occasion.

We'd made a record – at a cost of five pounds at a recording studio in Oxford Street – and he took it to Norrie Paramor, the show business manager. As it happened Norrie didn't have a pop group on his books, so we were invited for an audition. We walked out as if on air – he'd agreed to take us on.

Through his efforts we made our first record 'Move It' for EMI Records. It came out in July 1958 and went to Number Two in the charts and after that our success seemed to escalate.

It was an adventure and it brought in regular money – although on that first tour I was left with only twelve pounds a week after paying the others in the group.

When we stopped, everyone would run off in all directions and look for ten bob digs ... or we'd sleep in the bus.

It's great to remember those days. I remember a night we played in Halifax and the fans went berserk.

I think the fans then might have been slightly more mature but pop music is much more respectable these days. Basically, the fever is the same.

I can remember when hosepipes had to be turned on our fans. It was incredible.

Elvis Imitations.

I just wanted to be a pop singer, you know? I just wanted to put on me pink jacket, sing their songs, get all the glory, and that was it.

My voice was hardly broken then. That was my Elvis period, pompadour hair-style, all that. I was the rage of my school because I looked like Elvis. I even used to practise curling my lip the way he did.

Elvis was the guy I wanted to be like. He was the greatest. In fact, when I did my first TV show, the producer got me to get rid of my guitar and chop off my sideburns, because I looked too much like Elvis!

Anyway, even though I became a lot less wild than Elvis, I was still considered a rebel in Britain. After all, older people didn't accept rock'n'roll then the way they do now. So I'd have headlines in the daily papers like, "Is this boy too sexy for television?"

'Move It' was a smash hit record and therefore there was an immediate need for a follow-up.

We had no background. We didn't write our own material. 'Move It' was written by Ian Samwell and he'd written this other song 'High Class Baby.' When we went into the studio the magic didn't happen, and I thought, "Oh no, it's gonna be the end of a great career," and I went home and cried.

On subsequent tours we could afford to stay in first class hotels. For some reason though, it was never the same. We were never able to recapture the fun and excitement of that first tour.

Originally we were much more of a combined stage act than we are now. We were very young, we jelled, and we shared the same positive views about what we wanted to do.

I remember our passionately refusing to record 'Living Doll.' There was a day of telephone calls from Norrie Paramor, with me saying I hated the song and that it wasn't right for us.

"Why?" Norrie asked. "We don't like the way it's written – with a rock'n'roll beat."

"Change it," said Norrie. "Do it any way you like, but do it."

So we tried it country'n'western style and the number took on a completely new look. The record sold more than a million copies.

By 1962 I had appeared in my second film 'Expresso Bongo' in which I played a featured part. Then along came an offer to play the lead in a film musical 'The Young Ones.'

WITH GOLD MASTER FOR 'LIVING DOLL.'

You suddenly became aware that you were part of a property that was going to be fantastic and there was no doubt about it in anybody's mind.

I just feel that that was one of the most exciting times of my career because when we released the single – well, two weeks before we released it – the public had already had the publicity and the build-up was fantastic.

By the time we released it on Friday it had a million pre-sold ... and by Monday morning it was Number One.

Cliff's Conversion.

WITH HIS FATHER

I couldn't understand why a successful person should feel such a lack in his life, and I thought I might go to a spirit medium to try to contact my father, who'd died six months before.

Not that I had been particularly close to my father when he was alive; it was just that I wanted, if possible, to seek his guidance and to find out what was wrong with me.

When I asked Brian's advice he gave me a very definite "no" to the spirit medium. "Why not?" I said.

He opened the Bible which was always at his bedside and pointed to a passage which gives a clear warning against dabbling in spiritualism.

I was surprised and intrigued. I'd never read the Bible. I thought it was just an old book with no relevance to present-day problems.

I borrowed Brian's Bible and began dipping into it. I soon found that, so far from its being out of date, it contained a vast store of everyday wisdom.

It was the New Testament that really caught my attention. Not only was it the story of Christ. It was Christ speaking directly to me – something I'd never quite realised before.

I'd been baptised and brought up an Anglican. I'd been taught my religion in school but at fourteen I'd flatly refused to go to confirmation classes. I'd rejected religion, or rather I'd rejected what most people take for religion but to me seemed no more than lip service to the Christian code.

Now I was finding out for myself that Christianity meant far more. Indeed, that it meant a personal relationship with Christ, and through Him, a special relationship with my fellow beings. Christ was telling me that I could never find myself except through Him. That every time I did anything I did it to Him. That every time I was nasty to anybody I was being nasty to Him.

There followed two-and-a-half years of reading and thinking and talking to people of all denominations. Among the orthodox Christians I spoke to were two masters at my old school, which my youngest sister was now attending.

Since the death of my father, I'd become very parental towards her, and on Open Day I went back to the school to talk about her work, and met these two masters again.

In time I learnt from them that it was not sufficient just to believe in God. You had to live on a very personal basis with God, and the only way to Him was through Christ.

It meant rediscovering Christ personally, and it eventually came to the point at which, one day, I opened my mind and heart to Him and asked Him to come in.

It was like being reborn and it has been my main preoccupation ever since.

Cliff found God in bed...
I suppose I'm one of those people who went looking for fame and fortune. I found it, but I also found it just wasn't enough. I was looking for something else – and I found it in Christianity.

I found it lying in bed, actually. I just said to God, "Look, I know You're out there, so do You mind moving in and taking over my life?" (1979)

Fame Not Enough.

I basically went through a period of depression. No, that's too heavy a word, um, disillusionment with what was happening. Okay, I was having a great time musically. The 'Young Ones' was flying to Number One and everything was

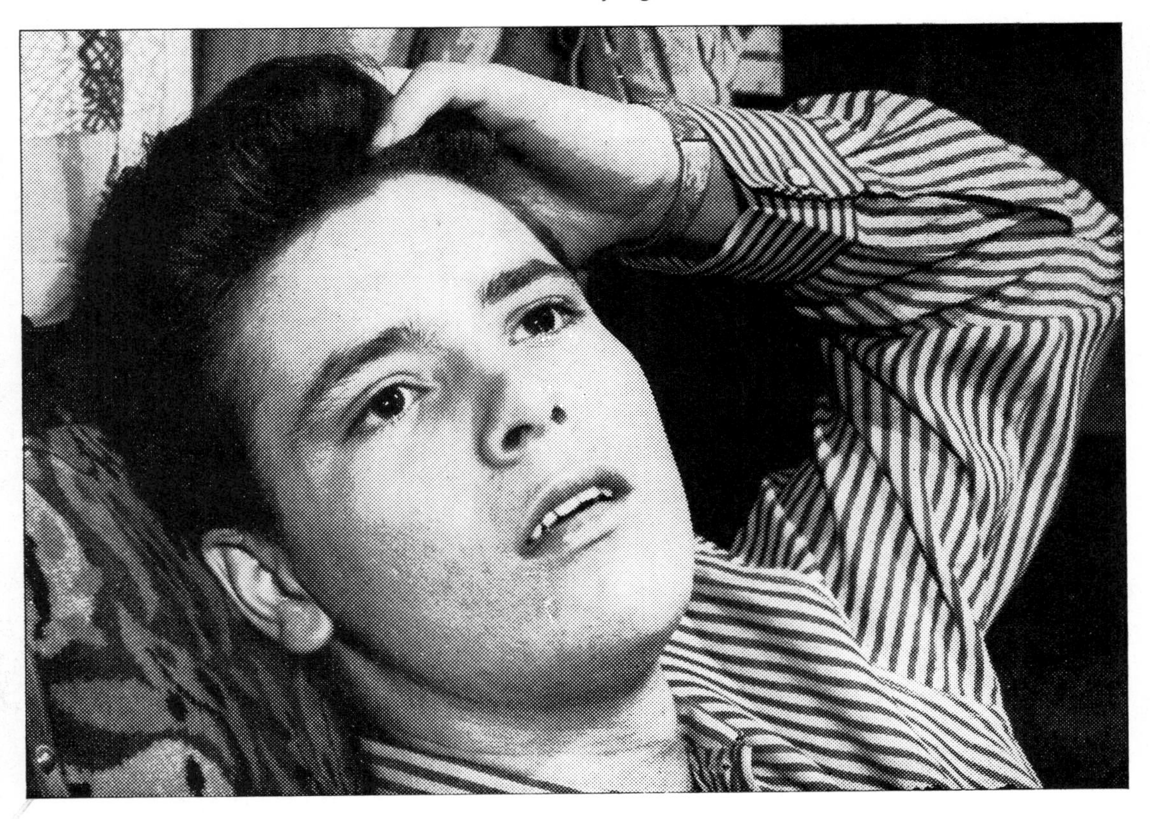

happening to me, so in terms of records I was at the height of my career and yet there was this feeling that things weren't right. I felt this couldn't be all I was living for and it just made me very serious minded for a time and I went round asking questions.

I spoke to some Jewish friends and spent two years with Jehovah's Witnesses. Religion kept cropping up in conversations, and after a lot of research I found there was a point in my life when I actually believed certain factors about Jesus Christ and God and I had to do something about it. I remember saying, "Okay, I succumb. Take me, I'm Yours." (1976)

A lot of people in this business go through periods of spiritual awareness even if they

reject it eventually. They get fed up with their material, fed up with fan worship; we all go through a period where nothing seems to satisfy us.

I mean me and the Shads had a terrific time on stage for an hour but there's another twenty-three hours to the day, and you begin to think, "Well, look I'm always on a lousy coach travelling to and from a show, is this it? Is this the glamour of it all?"

All I know is that the empty gap in my life has been filled since I became a Christian. (1976)

Cliff's mother married his ex-chauffeur, a man younger than Cliff…

It was the nicest thing that could have happened, both to her and to me. It didn't change our relationship at all. In fact, it was a great relief to me.

My father's death was a great loss to her and, although she married someone very much younger, he has been a stabilising factor.

Besides, I felt free to leave home and make a life of my own. We lived in Nazeing, Essex. We had quite a large house – it had previously belonged to the local squire. After my sisters and my

mother were married, however, there was nothing to keep me at the place.

At the time I was making a film at Pinewood called 'Finders Keepers.' It used to take me an hour-and-a-half to drive to the studios, which meant an uncomfortably early start every morning.

Bill Latham, one of the schoolmasters I mentioned, lived half that distance from Pinewood. He offered to put me up while I was shooting the film. I accepted and stayed with him and his mother for six weeks.

It so happened that they were going to move, so I said, "The three of us have got on very nicely together. When you move, may I move with you?" They were agreeable and we found a nice house in

WITH MRS. LATHAM AND HER SON BILL

Totteridge, North London, two roads away from Frankie Vaughan.

We've lived there ever since. Bill's mother has virtually adopted me; it's like having a second mother. (1976)

Of course, I keep in touch with my family and we have reunions. The family unit is the basis of the community and of peace and one must do everything to preserve it.

My family are Jehovah's Witnesses and, while I respect their viewpoint, I don't share it and we have great discussions. I'm always ready to talk with people about what they believe. (1972)

Two of Cliff's sisters became Jehovah's Witnesses during the time that Cliff was one himself...

Nothing would make me happier than for my family to become Christians, so that we could get back to being a family unit again – and that's the gospel truth. (1978)

The Christian Life.

I've thought things out. I used to shout my mouth off – I still do. But now I've got something to say. I'm in dire need of Christ. We're basically bad – all men are similar. You can be the Pope or the Queen. But as it says in the Bible, all men are sinners.

I could be a fake – a lot of people think I am. But I know I'm a Christian. So does God. That's all that matters. (1970)

I often sit back and think, "What am I doing in this situation." Like in Dublin, staying the night with three delightful old ladies. We couldn't relate to anything musically.

The only thing we had in common was a character called Jesus, and do you know what, that was sufficient. And I'd never have met those real, real people if I hadn't been a Christian. I'd have been playing Birmingham, earning bread.

It's changing fast in our side of the world. The very fact that Christians will be involved in a thing like this is an incredible step forward. They can see the value of good rock'n'roll and I'm really thrilled.

People like Larry Norman are the greatest exponents of rock'n'roll but all they do is Christian music. The general public don't know about Larry Norman but he's the guv'nor, writes incredible stuff. I do three of his songs.

It's the right use of rock'n'roll. In fact, Larry did a song called 'Why Should The Devil Have All The Good Music.' He had this thing about, "Why does the Church consider rock'n'roll to be sinful? It's great music. The Devil doesn't own it. It belongs to me." I tried to get him to come on my TV show but he felt it wasn't the right thing.

Some of the Church do look down on rock'n'roll but not the hip ones. Some people will continue to be shocked, in the same way that in Christ's time, He shocked people, right, left and centre.

We, as the young Christian section, have got to say, "Well, this is it. It's either us or the Devil that gets it, and we want it for God, so we're gonna do it, so you either come with us or get left behind."

I've made it clear through a thousand interviews where I stand as an individual, which is right down the middle. I'm a Christian who happens to be in show-business, and if the choice came tomorrow for me to leave showbusiness, I'd do it just like that. I know I could do it now, I nearly did it.

It's like the story of Isaac. Looking back, it seems to me that my one thing in life was my career. Now, the day that I took steps to give it up, I believe that's the day that God started saying, "Hold it, folks." But I believe I could give it up if I had to. God will make it pretty clear if He wants me to give it up. He has a way of doing that. (1976)

A Christian In The Music Business.

Where there's dishonesty and immorality, that's where Christians ought to be. But I don't believe that show business is more corrupt than other walks of life; it's just that we get more publicity. You'll find immorality among bankers, politicians, teachers, all the "respectable" professions, but perhaps they cover it up better!

I did think of getting out of it all about four years ago, so that I could go into religious teaching. I wound everything up and was accepted by Trent Park Teachers Training College. Then I did a film for the Billy Graham Evangelist Organisation and I changed my mind.

I realised that Christians are needed everywhere and that to quit would be like a rat leaving a sinking ship! And I certainly didn't want to feel like a rat.

Probably there aren't so many Christians in show business as elsewhere. So it's up to those of us who are in it, and have a bit of success, to stay there if we can. (1972)

It's no more difficult for me than for anyone else. I think if you look around, it's just as

hard to be a Christian anywhere in this world.

You see, the whole world is loose and immoral. You'll find immoral bankers, immoral estate agents, immoral teachers, and even immoral vicars. There isn't a career or a job that's clean from it. (1972)

Pop singing has now become a secondary part of my life. My faith in Christianity is much more important and the ability to spread the word of Christ means more to me than anything. (1977)

God Cures Cliff's Back.

The Rev. David McInnes said a healing prayer...

We linked arms around each other's shoulders and he prayed that if it was God's will, my back trouble would clear up.

About five days after arriving in Japan I threw away my painkillers. I felt so much better. And I really believe it was an answer to prayer. (1974)

Billy Graham.

I think Billy Graham has a job to do. Only a year ago, I heard, his organisation was getting more enquiries about the Christian faith than ever before. He's a man of great

intelligence, who is able to convey the Gospel of Christ in modern terms to a lot of people. I'd been a Christian for two years before I met him, so it wasn't he who first influenced me. But I admire him very much.

Do his campaigns have lasting effects? Obviously, but not on everyone. As to how many are influenced, I'd say, "God knows" – and I mean that literally. Certainly two or three per cent of those who came forward fifteen years ago are now ministers of religion. But one shouldn't be too interested in counting heads. (1972)

Bible Studies.

Cliff helped to promote Kenneth Taylor's 'The Living Bible'...

It's a shame that masterpieces can be understood only by those who understand masterpieces. The Bible is supposed to be for absolutely everybody.

We are so frightened of Mammon. It shouldn't be our master, obviously, but you can't produce a thing like this without using what mankind has at its fingertips. It doesn't bother me at all. I think God is worth eighty pence. (1971)

Cliff's Image Of Jesus.

It's difficult really. I never think about it 'till anyone asks. It's hard to keep it away from the image of the long-haired gentle-faced man you see in pictures. It can't be that wrong.

Jesus was a man, and in those days they did tend to have longish hair and beards. I doubt if He was a pretty man or an ugly man, but an ordinary man. He'd have been physically right, maybe a great athlete. He wouldn't have been skinny like me, or fat like Cyril Smith, just an average man. The epitome of what man is meant to be.

However there was a physical thing for him to get over. He lived in a time when they walked everywhere so he'd probably have had a lot of corns on his feet. (1976)

Elvis Presley.

WITH SUSAN HAMPSHIRE IN 'WONDERFUL LIFE'

I realised that Pat Boone is to America what Frankie Vaughan is to Britain, and I suppose, in a way, I am to England what Elvis is to the States . . . and please believe me, I'm not trying to be big-headed.

But Pat is a very religious man; married, and one of the politest, kindest men I've ever met. Take Frankie Vaughan – the same sort of person. Elvis and me . . . we're different, yet both of us lead decent normal lives.

I nearly met him when me and The Shadows were touring the States a few years back. One night we were in Memphis and an old man came to the theatre door and said, "Hi, ah'm Elvis's pa, d'ya wanna come on over and see his place?" We all said in amazement, "Elvis's DAD!" So we all leapt off and saw his house.

Unfortunately, Elvis was filming in Las Vegas. When we entered his house we wiped our feet on an effigy of Elvis on a mat and inside there were pictures, and awards everywhere like: "Elvis Coughed Here In 1968." And he had all these gold discs, even for B-sides. It was amazing.

I'd really like to meet him, but not now, not the way he is. He's so fat. While I was in the States there was a magazine which had this terrible caricature of him on the cover looking dreadful. They gave him four chins and this great gut.

Someone said to me if he was around would you see him but I said no, I couldn't bear it, not how he looks. I'd be so disappointed. (1976)

I remember Elvis as he was – dynamic, good looking and exciting. The man who invented my kind of music. And meeting

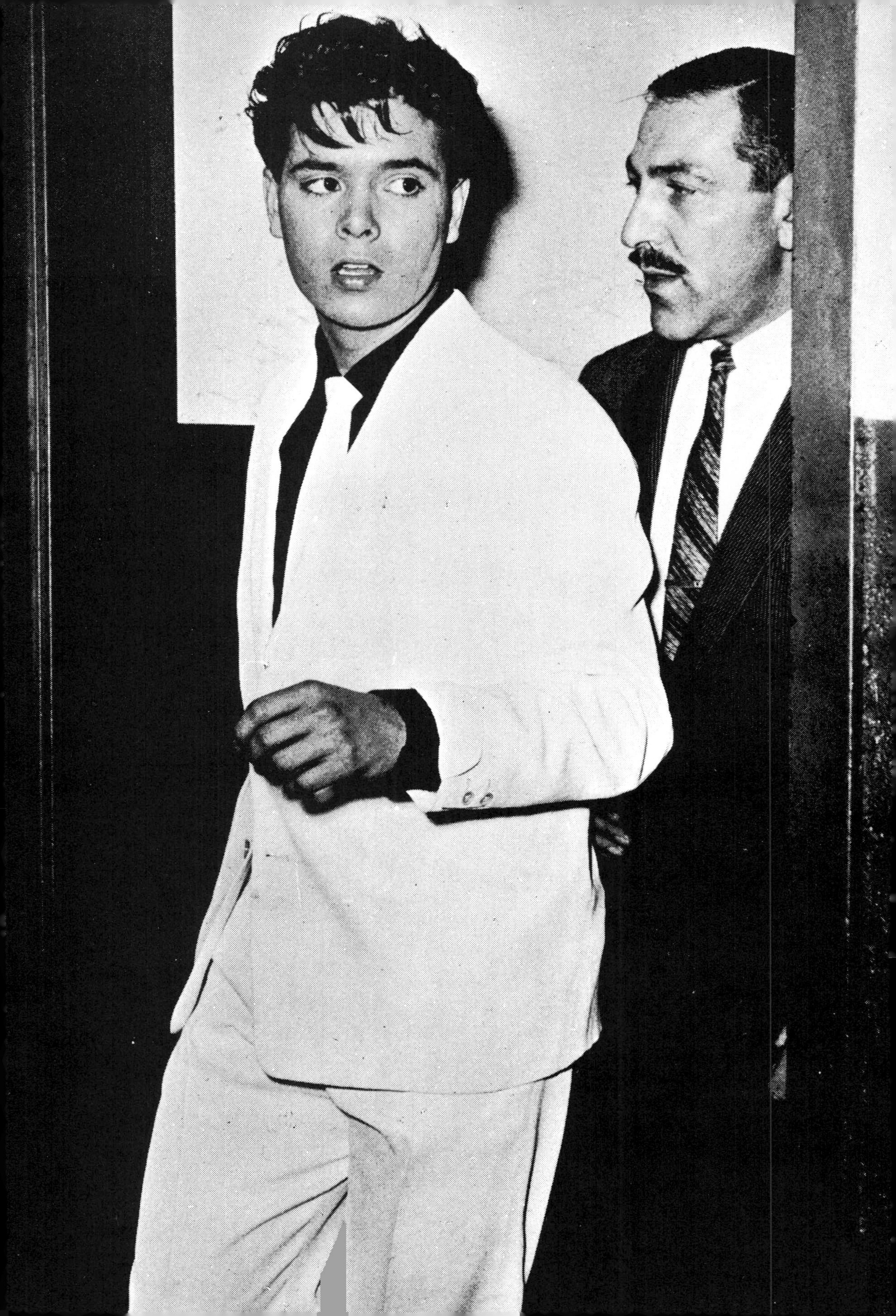

him the way he looks now would really shatter that illusion for me.

Now Elvis isn't too well and he's grossly overweight. There was a picture of him the other day in a paper and I just couldn't believe it was the same man. (1977)

I'm not so mad about his newer stuff really. I like some of the newer stuff, but not all of it. I don't like the live album material which he's been putting out, the spark seems to have gone from his performance. (1973)

It makes me squirm to think this is the guy I idolised for so long. He may have been the most successful artist, but as a man he never made it. I don't mean sexually, but just being a human being.

I didn't want to read that he picked up a girl out of the audience and within a week she was an absolute wreck on drugs.

Or about all the pills he was taking. Pills to make him thin, pills to make him fat.

When I think of what my sister and I went through all those years ago, with Elvis as our pinnacle, it's sad.

At Home With Cliff.

I tried living on my own once. Had a flat in Marylebone High Street, and, actually, I hated it. I couldn't *live* on my own. The idea of spending a whole day in the studio, then going back to an empty home... Awful.

Now I get home and everybody's in bed of course, but there's still *people* there, you know? I've got a *home* to go to. I've got a home. I still like to have a family life.

Food.

White sugar's really bad for you. It's the same as white bread. The stuff isn't even

baked – it's sort of steamed. My guitarist and his wife are vegetarians, and they bake bread like you wouldn't believe. There's a fantastic difference between home-made bread and the stuff you buy in shops.

I live with friends and they're not really into it at all. I don't want to force my own thinking down their throats. The lady who does all the cooking for me is like my other

DEZO HOFFMAN, REX FEATURES

mum. She's quite elderly, and she's not really into getting macrobiotic or whatever they call it. (1977)

Cliff's Weight Problem.

I actually used to be a bit fat. I'd never even thought about it till one evening I was sitting watching 'Coronation Street' on telly and Ena Sharples made a remark about "that chubby Cliff Richard." I was horrified! (1979)

So I immediately cut out all bread and potatoes and lost ten pounds in two weeks – I was 12st. 7lb. at the time – mind you I used to eat enormous steaks to make up for it. I love things like steamed pudding and great home-made apple crumble. I think people who tend to be fat love things like cream doughnuts.

I'm letting you into all my trade secrets, but yesterday I hadn't eaten all day and when I got home I found a Christmas pudding, cut off two slices, fried them up and ate them before going out to dinner.

I don't eat much during the week, but I let myself go at the weekend. Then I eat what I like. I put on three pounds last Sunday but got rid of it again by not eating on Monday. And last time I went on holiday, I put on ten pounds.

At one time I used to go around with a bag of apples and whenever I felt hungry I'd eat one. I didn't eat anything else, only apples. I really used to bore people with my slimming. But I don't suppose I'd bother if I wasn't in showbusiness. (1971)

I'm a one meal a day man and that keeps my figure. I also lie on my back twice a day and raise my feet a few inches from the ground and hold them for five seconds.

Inside me there's a Billy Bunter just burning to get out. He comes out quite often. On tour he escapes at weekends – I let him.

It works this way. On tour, I work from Wednesday to Saturday. On these days

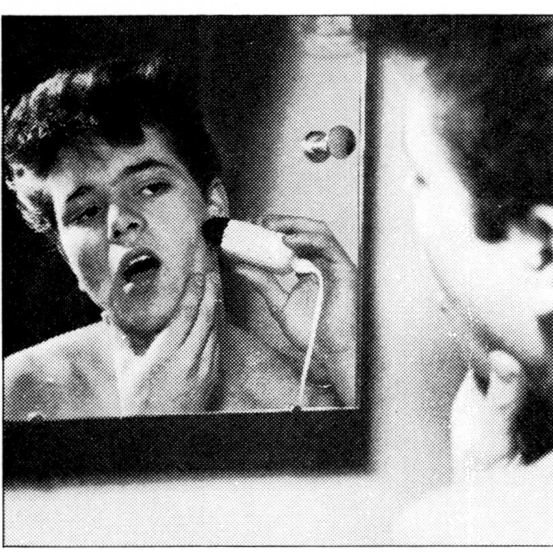

I have perhaps just a bowl of soup for lunch, and nothing before I go on stage. I have a meal after each show, steak or an omelette or fish.

On Saturday night, though, my biggest treat is to stop at a motorway cafe and have a real blow-out of eggs, beans,

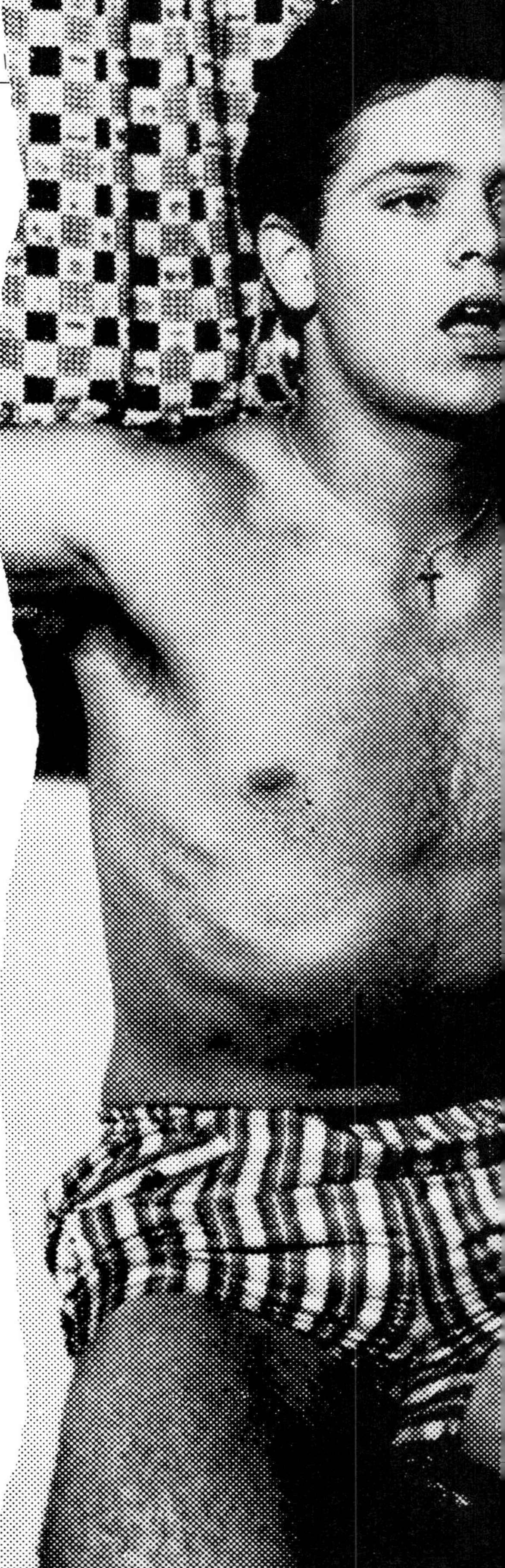

chips and a glass of milk. Wonderful! And all those stodgy puddings like spotted dick with custard ... Ooooh!!

On Sunday, I eat what I like. Then it's back to dieting on Monday morning.

On tour I make the boys laugh, because when we stop for a meal, I say,

"You just order what you like. I'll enjoy reading the menu." And I do. I look at it and say "Now this is what I'd have if ..."

But for those of us who like eating, there has to be the odd treat. You can't go on for ever denying yourself the things you like, but there has to be a balance. That's the true discipline.

I have to work to my own method. I know I can put weight on quickly, but lose it just as fast – almost half a stone in a weekend if I have to. So that keeps me at it. Motivation plays a big part. Knowing that three or four thousand people are going to be watching you on stage every night is a big incentive.

But even if I wasn't working, I think I'd still diet. I think I'd still like to be liked. To me, slim equals good-looking.

Growing Old.

I usually make light of how I look, but of course growing old worries me. I'm just lucky that all my family – particularly my mother – look incredibly young for their age and I seem to have inherited that.

I don't use stage make-up, for instance, I've never needed to, but I do worry about how my public would react to my getting old, so I do what I can to keep myself in shape. (1978)

Already, I feel if I wake up in the morning with bags under my eyes, I can't go out. And I'm frightened of smiling, because I've got a few wrinkles, you know. (1979)

Christmas.

I was converted in 1965, and now Christmas means more to me than just eating and drinking.

I always go to Communion on Christmas Eve, and although not all my family celebrate in the same way we do try to spend it together.

I remember the first year I took Communion on Christmas Eve. We were doing pantomime and the show finished at about eleven in the evening. Then I rushed off to the church in Finchley, near where we lived. (1979)

This year I've had a fantastic card done – I'm thrilled with it. It's a beautiful illustration of the Virgin Mary done by a girl from a spastic home, completely *typed* with her feet.

It was so good – better than most people could do with their hands – that I had all my Christmas cards made up in that design.

If you look very carefully at the card, you'll see that all down one side the word "love" is repeated, and on her robe is a passage from the Bible. I don't know if many people who received this card will notice – you really need a magnifying glass to read the words easily. But don't you think it's clever?

Why Cliff Never Married.

STILL FROM 'EXPRESSO BONGO'/BRITISH LION FILMS

Love & Marriage.

I try to ignore all the snide comments which are made about me simply because I'm not married.

I don't see why I should justify myself to the public all the time. Of course, I like women, and of course, I've known what it's like to be in love. I've had a couple of false alarms. The first time was with Jackie Irving, now married to Adam Faith. That lasted three years. (1977)

When I started to think seriously of marrying I didn't have a father to turn to so I asked my manager for his views. A big factor was how it would affect my career. Would I lose my girl fans?

That sounds strange today but in 1962 various pop singers nose-dived in popularity once it was known they'd married. He said, "Okay, go ahead if you want to."

Then I realised that by even asking the question I was expressing doubt...

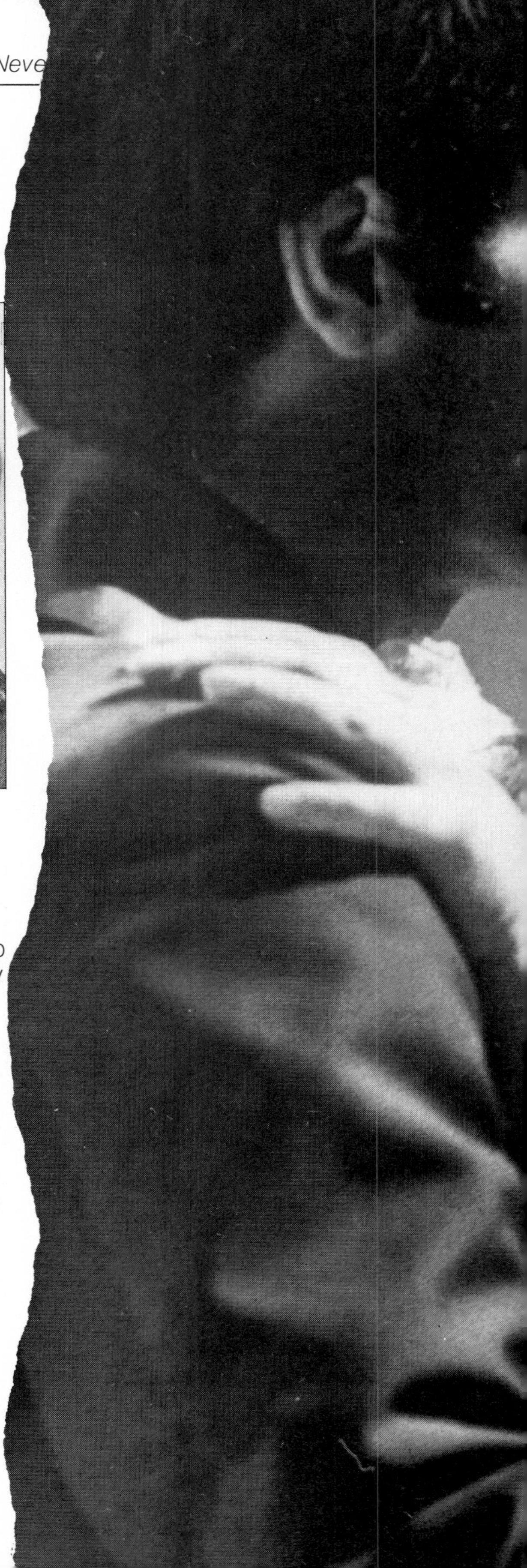

that I didn't love her enough to contemplate living with one person for ever.

I hadn't planned to be married or unmarried and I don't intend now to start planning in a positive way.

Marriage to me is a big important step and I don't intend to rush in because of any thought of being left on the shelf.

I love children and if I didn't get married I'd miss not having them. Let me make it clear that I'm pro-marriage, a wife, a family, home and loyalties. (1973)

The second time was with a dancer. That wasn't quite as deep a relationship.

I suppose I'm a romantic at heart, but when I see what's happening around me, it puts me off marriage. I'm surrounded by people getting divorced. If I were to marry it'd be for life.

But at the moment my life is as complete as anyone's can be. I don't think marriage would make it that much better. I'm surrounded by a lot of love, a lot of friends and I'm happier than I've ever been. (1977)

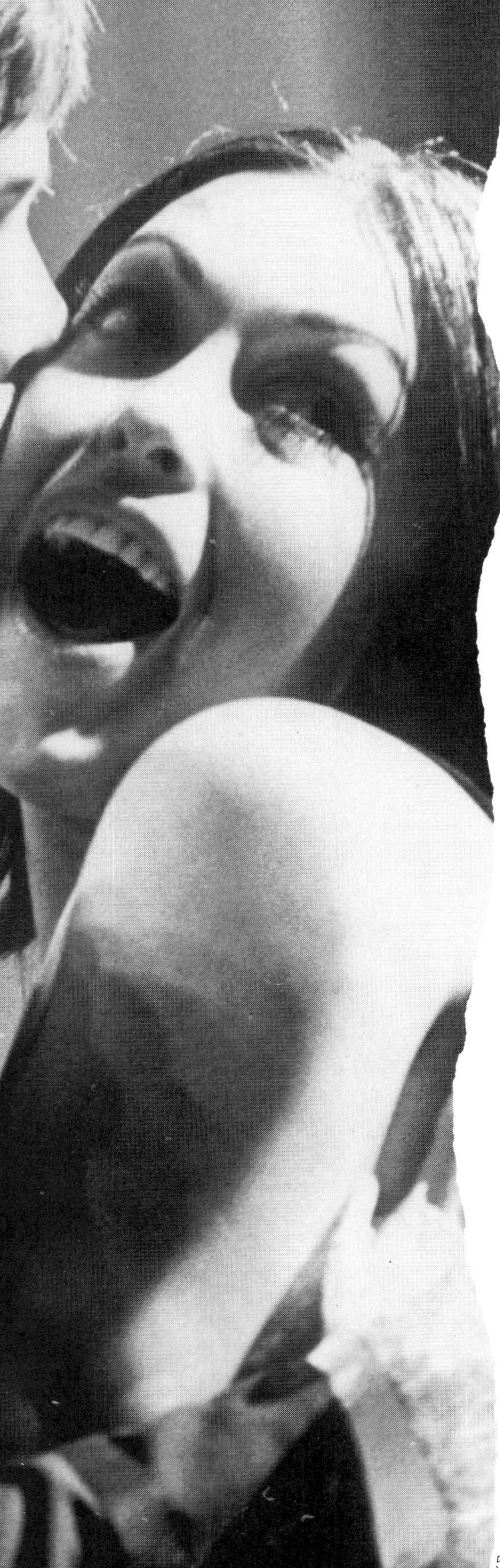

WITH MASSIEL/REX FEATURES

I used to worry when I saw Bruce and the other Shadows getting married. I thought, "What about me!"

But that feeling passed, for I realised you have to find the right person. Of course, I'd love to meet the girl of my life and get married. I'd like to have children, but as yet it hasn't happened.

Naturally, there've been plenty of rumours. At one time I'd only to be seen with a girl and the rumours would start flying. (1973)

I want to be married. I love kids, and would like to have some of my own.

And my mother is a bit anxious. She keeps introducing me to nice, single girls in that special way that mothers do. But nothing has happened yet. (1976)

I suppose bachelors are automatically regarded as lonely people and I've grown weary of those hoary old questions about marriage that usually have some built-in innuendo about homosexuality.

Maybe it's our mixed-up society that's conditioned us to suspect any adult

WITH SANDIE SHAW/REX FEATURES

who's single and over thirty as sexually abnormal. I don't know.

It's never seemed to be enough for me just to say I've never met the right girl. Well, it happens to be *true*. Even if I were

WITH OLIVIA NEWTON-JOHN/DEZO HOFFMAN, REX FEATURES.

some shadowy homosexual, which I'm *not,* I'm hardly likely to say so in any case! The fact is, I'm not whiter than white – at best I'm rather a dirty grey.

It's really all very simple. The idea of marriage and kids definitely appeals to me but I've got no urge to get married. Sad though it may seem, I'm actually the envy of some of my married friends, whose homes aren't half as relaxed and happy as mine.

Anyway, to be a Christian *and* to have a wife would be difficult for me. She'd get in the way; she'd change my lifestyle and turn me into a different person...

The strength and satisfaction you can get from being a Christian is more than you can get from any relationship... (1978)

With regard to Olivia Newton-John, she's a lovely girl. I think the world of her and like her very much, but she's not a girl-friend. Actually she already has a boy friend, so we won't be marrying, although we do socialise when she's in London. Sweet girl. (1973)

Everybody thinks I've got something against it just because I've stuck out longer than everybody else.

But to me marriage is vital, so important that I'm gonna have to want to be married. I'm gonna have to meet someone and be really in love with them before I get married.

I'm not just gonna get married to prove anything to anybody, and as I'm not in love with anybody I'm not married. That's basically it. (1976)

I think it unlikely I'll fall in love with a young girl. I don't believe in living together before marriage and I'd like to spend a lot of time with her family, and her with mine, before getting serious. (1973)

To a great extent it will have been pre-determined by God. I'll choose my wife; then having chosen, I'll realise that of course I didn't choose at all. When I look back I'll think, "Thank you Lord for leading me to her." It's as profound and deep as that. (1978)

If marriage isn't in the pipeline for me, then I'm not going to worry about it. My life is very happy and fulfilled as it is. (1979)

Dating.

I'm rather shy. It takes me a long time to pluck up the courage to talk to a girl. If a girl makes the first move I'm off. (1968)

This business of dating and what to do on a date is always a puzzle to me. I believe girls like to have their minds made up for them but I could be wrong.

Sometimes I've noticed one of my mates asking his girl what she'd like to do. Often the girl replies, "Don't know. What would you like to do?"

Now I believe girls say this because they don't know how much money the

boy has so she doesn't like to say what she'd like to do in case he can't afford it.

When I've dated a girl, I've usually planned the evening. A meal and a flick. It's no good my suggesting taking a girl dancing because I can't dance. No, honest! I can jive but that ballroom dancing stuff is not for me. So I guess the girl that I marry will either have to teach me dancing or not be all that interested in it.

Sex.

God built a sexual world – sure. Sex is everywhere. He built men and women and gave them to each other, and that's beautiful. It's fantastic.

But it's something that I feel should be kept special, and special for me means marriage. (1979)

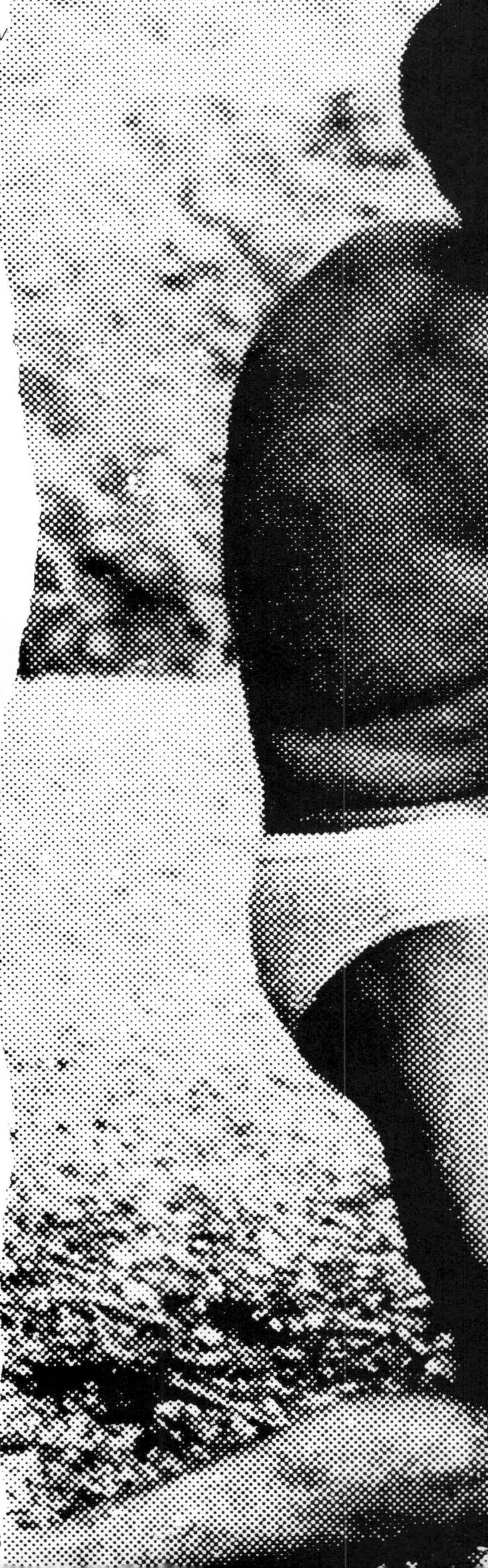

As a Christian I don't believe in extra-marital sex because God says it's wrong and I have to assume that HE knows better than I do. I don't sleep with women at all now – not since my conversion.

The Bible has very explicit things to say about it so that if you do burn with desire and need sexual relationships don't fight it, get married – that's what it's there for. Get married because you are allowed to enjoy sex, you are allowed to enjoy a happy marital state.

It's natural that a man is attracted to a woman and vice-versa. If you get a male

singer, females are going to enjoy that personality on a superficial sexual level.

But I don't believe that all those women who are at my concerts just want to leap into bed with me.

There are some attractive young women at my church and if you start talking with them it's sexual because you're attracted by their feminine personalities and you have the same effect on them but it's sexual in the purest sense of the word.

I'm very, very aware that the world is sexual. There are lots of women whose company I enjoy but there's no one who I have a burning desire to marry and have children with. But my life is very exciting, and I'm completely happy.

Homosexuality.

Crumbs, we all know homosexuals, don't we, nowadays? It's incredible, but we do. But homosexuality in my mind will never be *normality,* because I can see that what normality means is man and woman and procreating. I mean, I feel very straight about marriage, I've always held it in great awe; because, to me, it's vital. I've never had any plans *not* to get married. It's just that I don't *need* marriage at this moment in my life. (1976)

I was at a Christian conference in Morecambe, and I was asked to go to a Christian meeting in the town. I went along, and got a message that the Gay Movement were coming too.

I couldn't believe it. It was the first time I'd really come into contact with it, and they came flying in with make-up, and chiffon robes, and just generally screamed about the place.

That was my first dealing with them. I met a couple of them afterwards and one of them – the only one that seemed genuine – apologised for their behaviour. I said, "Well, don't you see you're doing it the wrong way?"

So we agreed to meet again, and when I got home I wrote a letter to this guy – I can't remember his second name, but

DEZO HOFFMAN, REX FEATURES

I think he was called Quinton something – and arranged to meet them again. Only this time, the stipulation was that there should be no press around. I got some of my Christian friends to agree to come along – some of them were scared stiff, because they'd never normally have met any of these people – they were willing to do it, but it never came off.

I was really disappointed, because I'm all for causes, where people are willing to get up and say something. It was patently obvious to me that these people were just not genuine.

I hate the word gay for a start. I've read books on homosexuality and they're very educational. They really give you an insight into what homosexuality is all about. It's not guys camping around, it's about men who have a feminine tendency sexually. It's got nothing to do with pansying around and getting into clothes – that's another thing.

It's vital that we understand the homosexual thing, both in women and men, I read a couple of books on it when all this happened, because I thought, "Crumbs, how can I talk to these people and answer their questions when I don't even know anything about it?" But I don't think these people are helping their cause at all. Not one iota. (1977)

The Gay Liberation Front picketed the inaugural meeting of Mary Whitehouse's anti-porn movement...
They were dressed up like nuns and screaming like banshees. They need a birching. (1976)

David Bowie.

I really like David Bowie. That album, 'Ziggy Stardust,' I thought was great, but I can't believe it didn't have a bad effect on the kids. I mean, he was purveying homosexuality, that's what it was all about. That sort of image and power is very dangerous. (1979)

Here's a genuine, married man dressing up as a woman. The impact is not on people like myself, or those in my age

DEZO HOFFMAN

group, but on the youngsters who will be tomorrow's people.

What will those ten- and eleven-year-olds think of someone who's a man dressing up as a woman at a pop show? Danny La Rue is different. He's a female impersonator, getting laughs.

But what is this Bowie man-woman image on the stage doing to young people? He upsets me as a man. There's a great responsibility all of us singers have to the ten-year-olds and some of us aren't living up to it.

What do some singers need all their trappings for? I get perturbed just thinking about it. Some of these people have fantastic talents, but they ruin the whole thing on a human level by being ridiculous on the stage. (1973)

I have this feeling that we've got to shoulder our responsibilities and realise we do influence people and can blow a lot of minds.

For example I never liked the Ziggy Stardust era with David Bowie because here was this guy coming on dressed as half-man half-woman before an audience full of thirteen- and fifteen-year-old kids. Now, how do we know what kind of effect David Bowie is going to have on them in later life?

Those are the people who are influenced by the world of arts today. They're certainly influenced by Bowie, definitely influenced by The Rolling Stones and if that's what's being created, count me out. I'd rather be clean and have no hits. (1977)

Cliff's Moral Code.

STILL FROM 'EXPRESSO BONGO' / BRITISH LION FILMS

Drugs.

If I hadn't become a Christian who knows what could have happened. I might have switched on to something else – drugs or whatever.

I don't see why I should have necessarily missed that but I did. The turning point was in Finchley twelve years ago. I said, "OK Jesus, I know You're there, come on in." (1977)

No one has ever offered me any drugs and I've never felt like taking any. I suppose aspirin is the nearest I've got to it.

The thing is I don't need drugs, nor does anyone. When I see other artists throw their lives away I feel so frustrated. (1968)

Maybe I would have wanted to escape, but I don't smoke and I think that this has

DEZO HOFFMAN, REX FEATURES

been a big help because the chances of my being offered hash were less. And hash is part of the drug culture you can be drawn into.

Drink.

It was in Italy that I got drunk the one and only time in my life. We were sitting out one evening and I was thirsty. Ronnie and Tony were drinking wine and they offered me some. At first I refused but then they told me how thirst quenching it was; I believed them and took a glass.

Whatever anyone tells you about wine quenching your thirst, don't you believe them. The more you drink, the more you want.

Before I knew what had happened, I was tight! And was I ill?! (1960)

Swearing.

People won't believe it, but I used to swear like a trooper. I was like everyone else at that time. And like a lot of people now.

Nowadays there's a loose feeling towards morality, but the way I found that

I could start to change myself was to say y'know if Jesus were standing right by me the last thing He'd want to hear was F-ing and blinding or whatever. Not only that, if my mother were standing beside me she wouldn't like it either.

I mean at that time every other word was "F."

I didn't need to say, "It's a F-ing great day," or whatever. So I used to say to Jet Harris, "Tell me when I swear." "Y'know," I said, "Draw my attention to it." I used to say it so often, I never knew who I was saying it to.

The thing about Christianity is it makes you become more aware. So consequently you begin to treat people with more respect. (1976)

Discipline.

Crikey, you have to be one of the boys and swear and sleep around before you're considered anything today, our society has become so twisted. And it worries me that the police are held in such scorn these days.

Again, it all comes back to the home. It'd be interesting to take a survey on the families that work and the families that don't and find out which ones have the discipline and the rod. (1976)

The Festival Of Light.

I don't know what they're doing now, but I would certainly support them. I think they'd probably approach me if they needed to.

The National Front? No, I didn't know they were associated with it. (1979)

Mrs. Whitehouse.

I don't care what people think. I think she's right. This world is in a pretty hectic state, our Western world anyway, and somebody has got to do something drastic. Mary Whitehouse is a drastic person. (1978)

I haven't seen any of Warhol's films, but as far as I'm concerned they stink of titillation. I saw a film recently about a child rapist 'The Offence.' It was violent and showed a man being beaten to death, but it was far more valid because of the impression it made. I can still remember the scenes vividly.

As far as I can see it's better to learn about sex from parents or by personal

WITH HIS MOTHER

experience. Mary Whitehouse and Norris McWhirter had every right to stop that film.

Mrs. Whitehouse is ten years ahead of her time. Cinema *is* being wasted. Morally, something has got to be done about it. There's a need for censorship. (1973)

I'd never take my clothes off. I can't see how it's necessary to go into detail over such matters. I saw 'Romeo and Juliet' – that had a bedroom scene, but it was done in such taste that there was nothing wrong.

The nearest I've ever got to that kind of thing was in a film I made for Billy Graham called 'Two A Penny'. In that there was some dialogue of that nature and some fumblings, but nothing more.

Often I think I'd like to see some pornography, but in my saner moments

STILL FROM 'SUMMER HOLIDAY'

I know I don't need to. I don't want to be turned on by anything except the person I love. (1973)

Television.

On 'The Rag Trade' TV Programme…
Do you know the entire programme was devoted to saying it was all right to pilfer – as long as everyone did it? I thought, "Ooh – how many people watch this and don't think what influence it's having on them?" I thought it was awful, bad, disgusting TV. (1976)

I remember one critic writing of one of my TV shows that it was so wholesome it made him sick! Well, fair enough, he didn't

WITH MILLICENT MARTIN/REX FEATURES

enjoy it – but it's a bit sinister when good and bad values swop places with everyone's approval.

Look, I'm very conscious that my TV shows go into millions of homes and that there are thousands of kids watching. As far as I'm concerned I want to show them that it's possible to be entertained *and* maintain Christian values at the same time. (1978)

WITH JANE MANSFIELD/DEZO HOFFMAN, REX FEATURES

Women's Liberation.

I'm all for opening doors for ladies and things like that. It's funny, because with my kind of work, I meet a lot of women who are

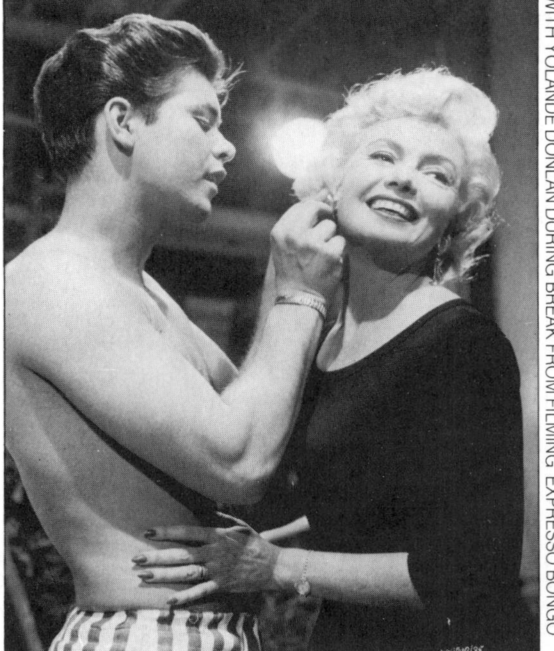

WITH YOLANDE DONLAN DURING BREAK FROM FILMING 'EXPRESSO BONGO'

very career minded and self sufficient. So, far from waiting for me to open doors for *them,* they open them for *me.* I really have to be forceful and make a point of opening doors for them.

Things like that make me glad there's so much old-fashioned romantic in me. It's nice to stand up when a woman comes into the room or to pay your respects to someone who's older by doing that, whether they be male or female. Or sending a bottle of champagne to a table as a mark of your admiration and affection.

Obviously, equal pay for women is a good thing. But what angers me about the women's lib thing is that they've made lots of women feel guilty because they're not company directors.

Nature says that women are supposed to have babies. What can be more important? Bringing up a child with love and affection is just as vital as doing a high-powered job.

The other thing is that there are definite differences between men and women anyway. It's impossible for instance, for women to play tennis as well as men do, because men are stronger.

I think we should get back to the old days with the man wielding his sword and protecting the woman. As a Christian that's what I honestly believe. (1977)

It's a joke, isn't it. I think it's ridiculous. I mean, women don't need liberating, they're quite free. Equal pay for equal work is a very right thing, it's justice, but you can't be liberated from your family, that's ducking out of a responsibility.

I'm old-fashioned enough to believe that there are responsibilities, you see. If there's a family it's the man's responsibility to work as hard as he can to keep

them, but a woman has a womb and that's for bearing children. (1973)

Politics.

I'm not a political animal. I can't decide which party I like – they all sound good to me. I worry a little bit about what is happening with the Unions, although I appreciate that people have a hard time to get by. (1977)

I'm not very up on politics at the moment but it's possible that I might go into it later. (1968)

Racism.

RAR, what's that? Oh, Rock Against Racism.

Well, yes I'm against apartheid, and that's why I go to South Africa, as my way of protesting.

But you'd be surprised how much things have changed there over the years. When I first used to go I couldn't play to mixed audiences, but that's all changed. Things are much better now, and it's such a beautiful country.

Some protests are so misguided. I mean, why try and stop this rugby tour when there's a mixed team? (1979)

Money.

I suppose my accountants would quite like it, but I'm definitely not a millionaire. I'm not even worth a hundred thousand pounds tax free. To be honest, I don't care what I'm worth. All I know is that the money comes in and I support – up to my ears – a charity known as TEAR fund (The Evangelical Alliance Relief Fund).

In any case I wouldn't want to be a millionaire. For a Christian that would be a dangerous state to be in. It means you've got a million pounds in the bank tax free. By all means keep something of it in the bank, but most of it ought to be out doing something for God's benefit.

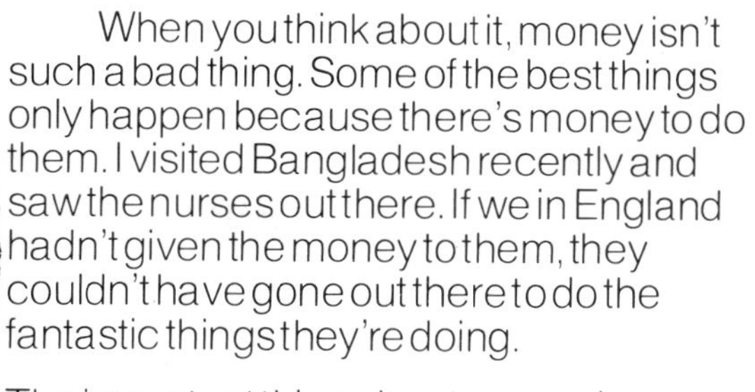

When you think about it, money isn't such a bad thing. Some of the best things only happen because there's money to do them. I visited Bangladesh recently and saw the nurses out there. If we in England hadn't given the money to them, they couldn't have gone out there to do the fantastic things they're doing.

The important thing about money is our attitude towards it. Whether we hoard it or whether we use it selfishly. I like to think I don't use it selfishly. I do concerts and I've done an album for the TEAR Fund. And whenever I do Gospel work I make sure I never receive any money for it.

I suppose if I turned my mind to it, I could earn a great deal of money. No doubt about it, because all I've got to do is only those things that pay a lot. I reckon if you gave me five years I could become a millionaire. If I really set out to do it. But I just couldn't see the point of it.

I think I'd find it harder to deal with poverty now, having known wealth, than I would have done years ago. What I'd miss most would be the luxury of being able to write a cheque for a certain amount of money at any moment.

It would take some getting used to. But I reckon I could get a job that would earn me thirty pounds a week, so I wouldn't be totally lost.

Of course I've got Christianity to help me now, so I know I could cope. I'd never be abandoned by God. (1974)

I've been praying for a long time that God would help me use my money correctly.

Maybe it will come to a point where I'll just sign away everything as I earn it. I'm quite prepared to do that if God tells me. (1974)

I believe in tithing. I don't know how the Osmond Brothers quite work out their tithe, because when I go to my accountant I find it extremely difficult to understand it. But I do feel that my money should be used for God's work, and therefore I do use a great deal of it. I don't know exactly how much; whether it's ten percent or more likely twenty percent. (1972)

The Music.

ON 'OH BOY!' T.V. SERIES

Performing.

I want my music to be heard. The words are important and I think people enjoy themselves more if they are sitting down in comfort. (1979)

I've always considered myself a hairy rocker.

Rock'n'roll is always changing. It's not just Jerry Lee Lewis. I mean, I love all that but I love the new people too. Elvis Costello and The Police. Rock'n'roll isn't just a tempo, it's a culture; it spans from just right of Max Bygraves to just left of Led Zeppelin. Someone recently called me a musical parasite, but that's ridiculous. How can I be a parasite when me and the Shads started it all? What the devil do I sing if I don't sing rock'n'roll? (1979)

The fans get very upset if I don't do 'Living Doll' so I do it even though I don't *enjoy* doing it. At one concert I did it as an introductory number and it went down so well – perhaps that's the answer.

At one stage I dropped a lot of my hits from the show, but the audiences went away disappointed so I put them back in.

As there are rather a lot of my hits I choose different ones to do for each tour – but I make sure that at least thirty per cent of the show is hits.

I know that a lot of people have given up doing their old numbers, or do them either halfheartedly or in a medley, but I think that's wrong. The people come along expecting and hoping to hear them, and go away disappointed. I think that's very sad – Diana Ross did it in her show, dealing with all those Supremes hits in about ten minutes and it really upset me! (1976)

I have this thing about volume. When I went to see Elton John in Sheffield, it was much too loud. He has a really good band with him, but I couldn't actually hear any of them properly until I went outside and listened through the open door!

The whole point, as far as I'm concerned, of this new sophisticated equipment is that you can control the sound and the distortion – so why is so much volume needed? (1976)

Gospel Concerts & Religious Songs.

I really don't know what I'm doing out there half the time. I just trust in the fact that my motives are right, and I want it to be right.

My motives are multiple. I want to raise money for charity. There are many

people who I think will benefit from being Christian, from knowing what I know. And it's not my secret. It doesn't belong to me.

To be able to sing and speak about Jesus, at any time, is to me a great privilege. There must be millions of people who would give anything to have a platform to spout about whatever they believed.

I'm not misusing my platform. I still have a responsibility to those who don't want to come so I do a secular tour. I do a smattering of Gospel stuff in that, but I choose material that I think is valid musically, so nobody minds.

The reason I separate them is that there are people who don't necessarily want to go and hear Gospel music, so by advertising a Gospel concert, anybody that comes knows they're going to hear Gospel music, so therefore I'm being legitimate.

There's no other real reason for separating them. Musically, all of it stands up. What I've always tried to do is just be as real as possible and share myself. But the concerts I've enjoyed most have been the ones where, when I've left the concert, I know a little bit more about the audience.

Now the Gospel concerts give me a hundred percent opportunity to really share what's deep inside me. I snatch at

WITH THE SHADOWS/DEZO HOFFMAN, REX FEATURES

bits that come into my mind and talk about it for a little while, interspersed with songs.

Yes, it's allowing myself to be used. A lot of people say that in a detrimental way, but that's exactly what a Christian ought to be, open for use. But not for misuse; I think I'm fairly intelligent, and I know when people are misusing me. People who *call* themselves Christians have tried to make use of me, but you can spot them a mile off. (1976)

Confounding The Critics.

There are journalists who don't like me, just because they can't put me in a bag. I refuse to be put in any musical bag. I don't want to do an album of all the same material.

It's interesting for me to make it as varied as possible, and I include rock'n'roll in what I do. But I might want to do a ballad after that.

When I compare the old with the new and the old 'Move It' and the new 'Move It' I can see that I've progressed. It's a terrific challenge for me to have a go at so many musical styles.

I did drift away from rock'n'roll for a while because I didn't want to record it all the time. The drift lasted for a few years but I'm back into it now.

I'd like to do an album of all the old numbers re-visited. We could use all the technical and sophisticated methods of today. I'll bet they'd sound fantastically different because everything is so sophisticated now.

It's no good trying to compete with the old stuff. Alvin's version of 'Move It' is not as good as the original. It has changed a lot. It probably *is* as good musically but there is no way that his version will ever have the nostalgia or the excitement of the original.

I'm not interested in doing my old songs chord for chord, just as they were on the records. I want to do them in the 1975 style and they'd still be good because I wouldn't be trying to recreate

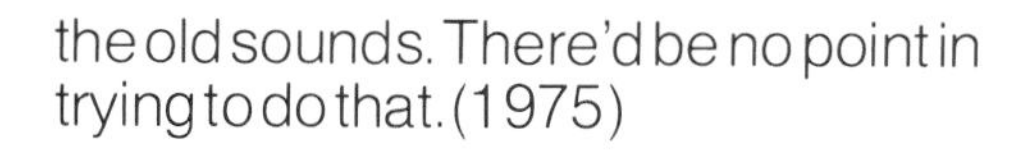

the old sounds. There'd be no point in trying to do that. (1975)

Songwriting.

I've never thought of myself as a song-writer. I'm an interpreter of other people's songs. I know you'll think this is crazy, but it wasn't until very recently that I even realised how much money there was to be made in songwriting. You see I've never really been worried about making money – I don't know to this day how much I earn.

When I've written a song it's mostly been for the kick I've had to see my name credited on the record.

It's discipline you know. I stopped writing years and years ago when I got more into performing. I helped to write 'Bachelor Boy,' 'Don't Talk To Him,' 'On The Beach' and two or three other things with The Shadows, but I just stopped, which was fatal.

I'm gonna go away to a little cottage in Wales, take my guitar and cassette and see if I can stick it for a week by myself. I'll

sit down for a couple of hours a day and write. I've just gotta discipline myself. (1976)

I find it hard to write songs, especially basic rock'n'roll songs, although theoretically they're the easiest. I find the ballady, poetic numbers much easier.

I think I've only ever written one song which came easily. It's called 'Night Time

REX FEATURES

Girl' and was motivated by a girl we know who needed, and still needs I suppose, help. She used to lurk outside my house all the time, and once she actually broke in. She's not a thief or anything, but rather disturbed.

The song, probably because it was motivated by personal experience, just simply flowed out. I finished it in an afternoon. But that was a rarity. My problem is that I've got no discipline; the sun comes out, and I go into the garden to water the roses or something!

I did once go down to a cottage in Wales for a whole week on my own. Just me, my dog and my guitar. I thought I wouldn't be able to stand it alone, but I loved it. Yet all I got done was a verse of one song, and I started on another which I still haven't finished. (1976)

I did have three or four songs on my gospel album, 'Help It Along'. I find Gospel songs very hard to write because I'm always conscious of them sounding rather trite; and ones I write I feel have to stand up as songs in their own right.

I'm also over-sensitive about those songs, because Christianity is a subject I feel so strongly about. So I spend a lot of time scrapping gospel songs. There is one particular number called 'Yesterday And Forever' which I spent months on,

"cleaning it up." I'd written it at a time when I was very upset, because every time I appeared with other Christians I was knocked by the public, yet George Harrison could sing 'My Sweet Lord' or James Taylor sing about God and everyone thought it was great. (1976)

Producing.

I like producing – I expect it's the feeling of power! I'm dead scared of the responsibility, but I do feel that even with good songs and a good engineer you need someone to be objective and give guidance. So that's what I try to do.

Underground Bands.

I like a lot of the underground bands but I can't understand why they feel they have to appear on stage looking like a bunch of tramps.

When people pay good money they expect everything to be just right, including a well turned out appearance.

I wouldn't feel my best unless I went on stage looking smart. (1971)

New Wave Bands.

It's no good the New Wave lot coming along thinking they're doing something new – they're not. We were doing it eighteen years ago, and Elvis started it all off before that.

What we've got now is the first generation of forty-year-olds who dig rock'n'roll. When I was eighteen, people of forty hated rock. Now when we're sixty ... it may sound ridiculous, but I'm going to love rock, the music will still be our music. (1977)

Some, like Tom Robinson and Elvis Costello, are great, but most of them are lousy. And I find it all a bit repulsive that people should want to look so ugly.

The punks think they own the pop scene, but they forget they're just leasing it from us. (1978)

Acting.

No singer has managed to bridge the gap between pop and the theatre and I want to be the first to do so.

But I'll never give up pop. I love it. Singing is the easiest thing for me next to getting out of bed. But I find acting very fulfilling. (1971)

WITH THE SHADOWS/DEZO HOFFMAN, REX FEATURES

STILL FROM 'EXPRESSO BONGO'/BRITISH LION FILMS

I want to do so much in the acting field. I've made films, but I'm never happy with them once they are completed.

I'd like to go for something completely different, like making a horror film, with me playing the Dracula-type lead. But television acting is hard for me, because you have so many distractions. (1968)

The play 'Five Finger Exercise'...
The play I did last year was one of the most exciting things I've done in my career so far.

I'd wanted to act very much and we let this fact be known. When I was offered

WITH SID JAMES

STILL FROM 'EXPRESSO BONGO'

the part, I thought, well, I may as well jump in the deep end.

It was the old play 'Five Finger Exercise.' Although it wasn't an original I really had something to do. I had to act and I had to get out of myself.

It was super because we got some fantastic press really, even papers like The Telegraph and The Times were nice and they don't throw their compliments away. They said good things about it and I felt really quite proud. (1972)

REX FEATURES

The movie 'Take Me High'...
It's really quite different from the other ones. In the other films there was always The Shadows or Una Stubbs. This is the first time with a completely new team.

We all got on fine. It was great working with people like Hugh Griffiths – Debbie Watling, the leading lady, she was really lovely.

We've made it for all the family. There's nothing in it that would be smutty or embarrassing. People can just go out and have a nice evening. (1974)

I play a kind of sharp merchant banker who moves into Birmingham – the last place he wants to be – and falls in love with a girl.

The actress is Debbie Watling. How old? Oh, in her twenties. She's fantastic.

We kiss in four different ways for about half-a-minute. The cameras merge this into one big kiss. It's a fabulous kiss and was all my idea.

WITH UNA STUBBS/DEZO HOFFMAN, REX FEATURES

We exchange kisses all the time, but we treat that love scene rather beautifully. It's that old-fashioned falling in love. A scene where people still like holding hands together.

Boys and girls tend to do that on the sly now, or else they don't talk about falling in love. That's when I say to myself they're really missing out. (1973)

On 'Two A Penny,' a film made for Billy Graham…
I don't actually become converted at the end of the film. We felt that would be a bit *too* much, but the audience is left with the feeling that I could be and I'm made to concede that there *may* be a God. I put a lot into 'Two A Penny' and had a hand in the songs.

I feel they didn't judge it fairly as an artistic work, quite apart from the message. I think it's the best thing I've

IN 'ALADDIN' WITH SYLVIA SIMS/DEZO HOFFMANN, REX FEATURES

done on the screen. As for the message of Christianity, that seemed to embarrass them, but I don't think it should have done; after all, religion is an essential part of life.

Pantomime.

In 1966 Cliff played Buttons in 'Cinderella'...

Hugh Lloyd and Terry Scott were the Ugly Sisters, and off-stage we got on famously.

During the first show (the panto lasted two and three quarter hours and there were two shows a day) we'd have a tea break. One day I'd bring in some bread pudding my mother had made, then the next day one of the others would bring in something they'd got, and we'd all sit around talking.

Then in the evening during the "gin and tonic" break – although I'm not keen on gin, so I'd have a glass of wine – we'd sit and chat. It was all very pally – a social time, and one of my fondest Christmas memories.

I remember that on Saturday nights we used to use the stage after the pantomime. I'd hire a movie and bring in my projector and the cast would sit around and we'd have our own private film show. (1979)

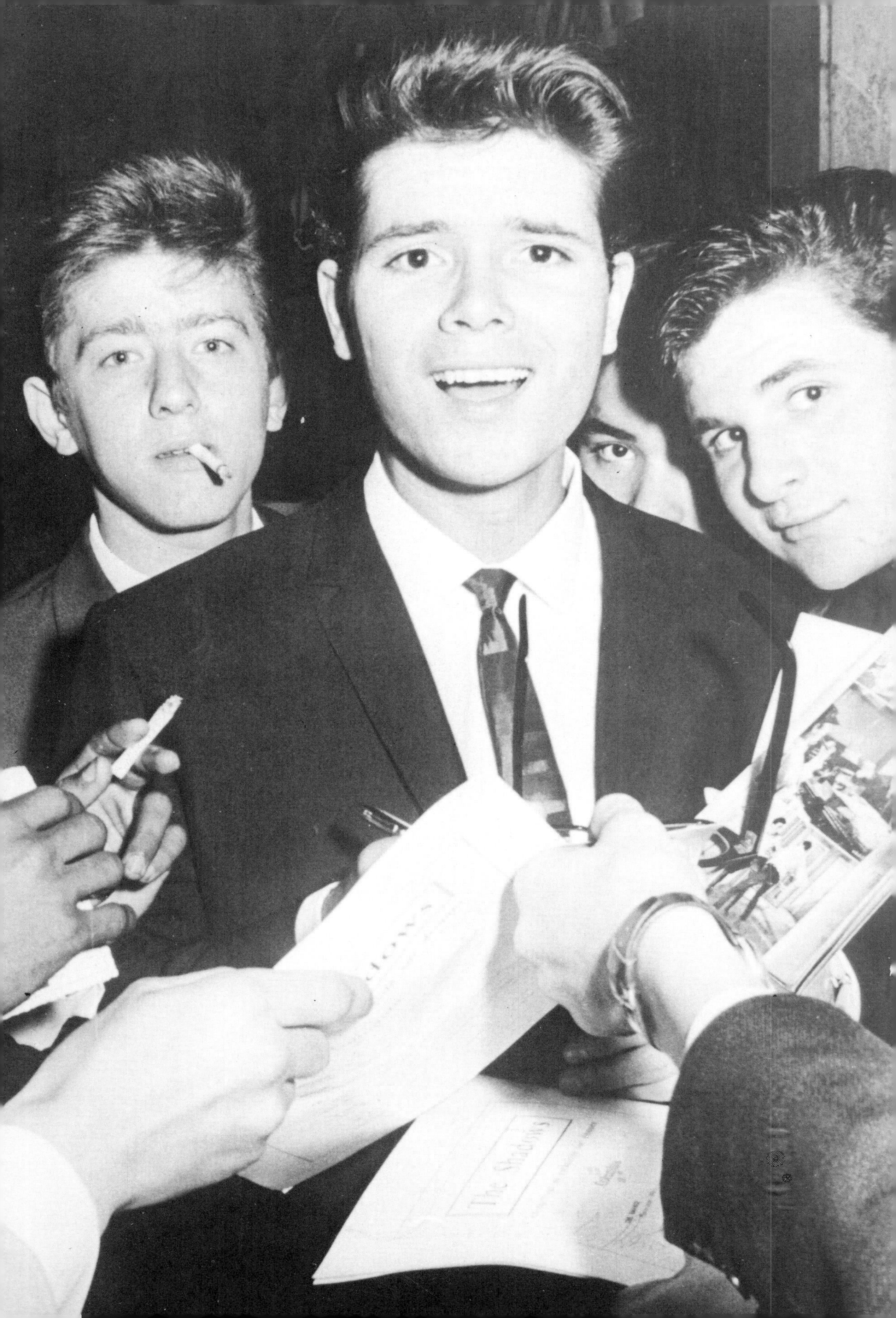
The Shadows

Fame.

I used to go out of my way to make the kids scream. Now they scream when they hear my name. (1959)

I don't mind signing autographs and I don't get tired of the fans either. It's natural to want to be liked and I enjoy it. You can't remain in show business without being an extrovert. I enjoy everything which goes with it – all the chasing around.

My mother used to say that when you're well-known you can't go anywhere; but you can, because you can afford to go places where you're not known, like America. It's absolute rubbish to say pop stars have no privacy.

It's a frame of mind. Of *course* you can do things like going into a pub. The thing to do is just to go in and have a drink. But if you walk in wearing a double-breasted mink jacket obviously people treat you as something different. (1971)

REX FEATURES

Oh, sure it's difficult sometimes – like when a fan turned up on my doorstep recently, with a couple of suitcases and announced she'd come to stay.

CLIFF RICHARD
AND THE SHADOWS
IN PERSON! HERE TUES 29 JAN 5-15

OMEGA
OMEGA

DEZO HOFFMAN, REX FEATURES

She said she'd been "told by the Lord" that I needed her, so at considerable personal expense she'd obeyed the Lord and there she was.

I tried to explain that I was surprised that the Lord hadn't told me what He had in mind, so that I could have at least prepared the spare room – but she wasn't impressed. It took a couple of policemen to get her out of the house.

Okay, it may sound funny, but I often find it really sad to encounter as many sick and lonely people as I do – some of them long past the teenybop age. (1978)

Some of them are downright rude! Once or twice I've had people interrupt me while I'm having a meal in a restaurant; slapping an autograph book down on the table and expecting me to sign it, while they look the other way, without even so much as a word. I don't sign autographs like that till they've asked me politely.

Or another time I got dragged off by a policeman to a nearby van before I had

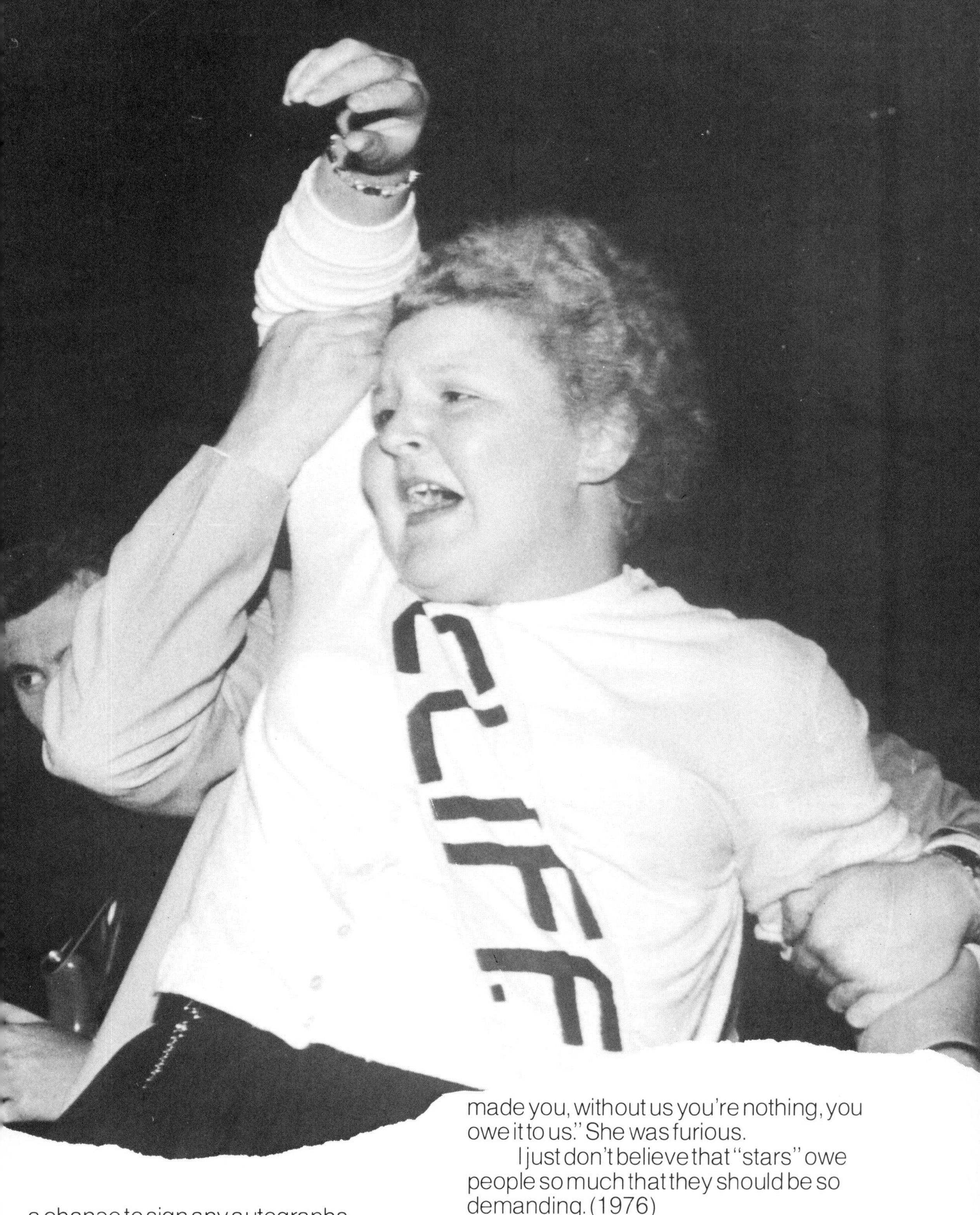

a chance to sign any autographs, because they were worried about my safety. One girl obviously wasn't though, all she cared about was getting my autograph. She went berserk when I wasn't able to sign, shouting things like, "We've made you, without us you're nothing, you owe it to us." She was furious.

I just don't believe that "stars" owe people so much that they should be so demanding. (1976)

I used to moan about being recognised all the time and things like that, but that was just immaturity. The one thing that I wanted really was the fame, and I've got it. (1976)

Show Business.

WITH JANE MANSFIELD/DEZO HOFFMAN, REX FEATURES

I didn't plan when I started singing professionally at the age of seventeen that I'd still be around now. But luckily it's happened that way.

I've always tried to keep in touch with my audience and retain a style of my own, and fortunately it's all coincided. (1976)

First I never thought I'd last more than five years. Then it was ten. Then I stopped timing it. I got into music after that and took things seriously. (1975)

I know you can't please everyone, even if you sell a million records – and I've done that several times – there are still fifty million people out there who didn't buy it!

So I reckon there are plenty of people who don't like me. But on the other hand I've had a twenty-one year career in this

WITH UNA STUBBS/DEZO HOFFMAN, REX FEATURES

business. So I can't have done anything *too* wrong, can I? (1979)

I've learned one very important thing over the eighteen years I've been in the business; now I'm proud to be commercial. People went out and spent money on my records, and that enabled me to do something now I might prefer artistically.

So I'd say, never knock them if you have hit singles – always play them and be grateful for them.

I've been very lucky in my career – I've been surrounded by a few honest

WITH KENNY LYNCH/DEZO HOFFMAN, REX FEATURES

people; I have always been with the same record company and have a very special relationship with them, and my office and musical associates are great, too. It's very conducive to being artistic. (1976)

Of course I could lead a totally showbiz life if I wanted to but I like to get out and meet

DEZO HOFFMAN, REX FEATURES

people who have nothing to do with show business. I find there's a lot of reality outside.

When I'm at home, I visit my neighbours' houses. Of course it takes time before they treat me as an ordinary person but you can't expect to be treated normally straight away.

I don't go to a lot of showbiz parties and I really don't mix with showbiz people. My closest friends are The Shadows, Una Stubbs and Norrie Paramor. (1971)

The one thing I'd criticise people for in the business is that they're terribly narrow-minded.

All they talk about is the business, and their record, but there's a place for all that. Everybody goes home except us, we seem to be the only ones who don't.

I've spent some really boring times with showbiz people. (1976)

AT THE ROYAL COMMAND FILM SHOW, 1960

The Eurovision Song Contest.

EUROVISION SONG CONTEST/DEZO HOFFMAN, REX FEATURES

The one country all other countries respect in pop music is England. They fear us, man. That's what makes the Eurovision so important.

I can't understand how people can criticise the contest if they don't enter songs in it first. There's a new system this year where anybody can enter a song.

What the contest needs is our best writers, people like Paul McCartney. 'Listen To What The Man Said' would have been a great song for Eurovision. So would that David Essex single 'Hold Me Close'.

It's the Maccas of this world I'd like to sit down with and talk the thing through to show them the potential of the Eurovision.

'Congratulations' came second in the contest in 1968. I was very disappointed that the song didn't win, but it sold more than the actual winner – in the end.

I've had two zonking great hits out of the contest, both of them selling over a million, so as far as I'm concerned it's well worth my while doing it. But I'll have to wait a while before trying again. Maybe in another five years.

I'd like to win it once. I still think we've been cheated every time. In both cases the record that won has not sold as many as our entry. And the contest's supposed to be picking out the best pop song of the year. Something's wrong somewhere.

England's always pretty high. We're consistently in the top five. It seems to me a little unfair. I can't help but think that there's a little bit of feeling against us. I just hope that Olivia's going to do the same thing this year – and that if she loses, her record will still sell more than the winner. (1974)

The Songs.

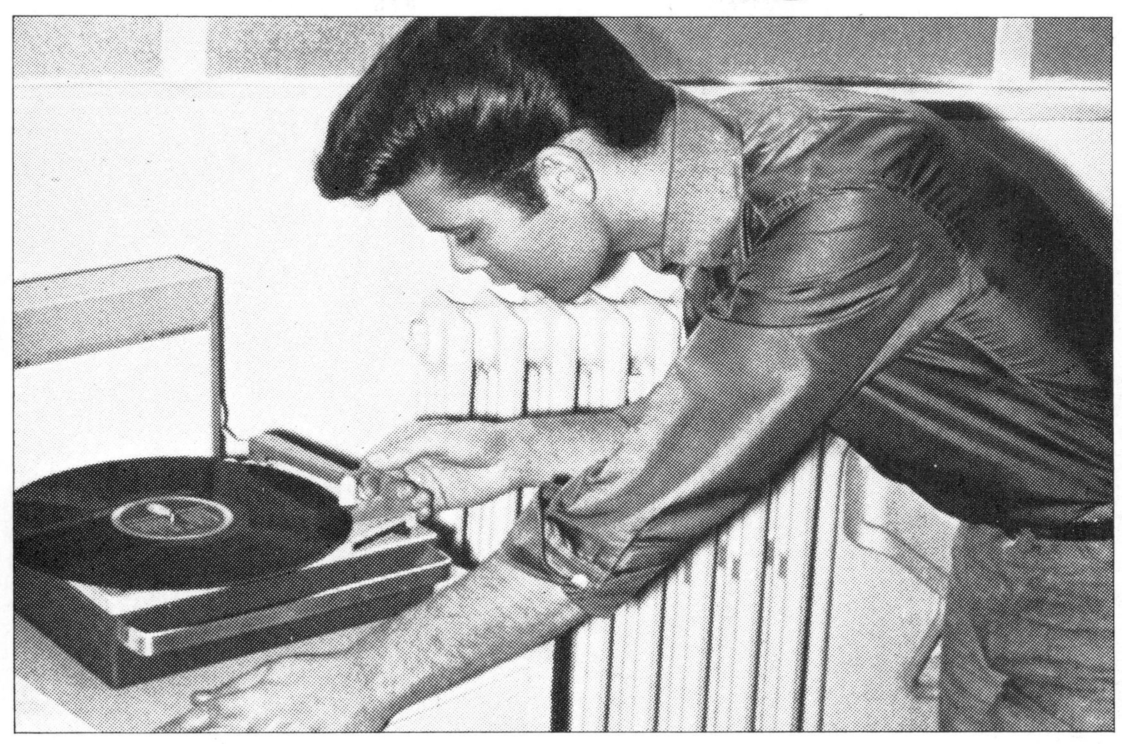

Good rock numbers don't grow on trees. They're hard to find. (1960)

'Living Doll.'

We all hated the song at first. It was in the film 'Serious Charge' and I hadn't read the small print, which said we had to issue it as a record.

Bruce Welch had the idea of making it a country kind of song and we did it in three takes one Saturday morning. (1978)

'The Young Ones.'

I think it was the peak because I'd never ever sold as many records so quickly.

'The Young Ones' was released as a single on the Friday, but prior to that we were being told that the advance orders were two hundred thousand. The advance orders were three hundred thousand and by Friday when it was released there was a million orders. By Monday morning it was a Number One.

And it's never happened to me since. (1976)

'Brand New Song.'

I've had my first flop in fourteen and a half years.

'Brand New Song' is my first record not to get into the charts. I really can't understand why, because I played it to my mother and she was sure it'd be a hit. (1973)

'Honky Tonk Angels.'

I hope it's a flop. I never want to hear it again and I hope most of the public never hear it.

I knew honky tonks were something to do with bars but I completely misconstrued the meaning. Okay, some

people might say I'm naïve. Obviously, it's very embarrassing for me.

Now I know what I've been singing about, I've taken steps to do all I can to make it a flop. I hope no one buys it.

It's too late to get the record withdrawn because it has already been distributed by my record company all over the country. I heard it on the radio eight times in one day last week, so you can imagine how I feel.

If the record is a hit and I'm asked to sing it, I will refuse unless all the words are changed. (1975)

'Every Face Tells A Story.'

The album took about five weeks. We've basically worked on it non-stop since we came back from Russia.

We are very quick, much quicker than most. We keep hearing about people taking four months over an album but we know basically what we want – whereas a lot of people go in the studios and don't even know what songs they're going to do.

I sing in the vocal back-ups. That always helps on the general tone of the record because I always think the best sound is when you sing with yourself. It means the texture's the same, plus it adds a certain warmth.

I usually sing straight. There are three songs I know of where we double-tracked for effect.

My voice has got better over the years and, well, I'm more cheeky with it now. I've been singing like this for about three years. I keep saying I've been one step ahead and now they've all caught up. (1976)

'Miss You Nights'

I think it's one of the nicest songs I've ever made. A guy called Dave Townshend wrote and recorded it and when I heard his version it was terrific, so we just stole the whole thing. He was pleased to have that happen. I mean it could've been anybody. It would've been a hit.

What I hope 'Miss You Nights' has done – well, what I know it's done – is that the hairy groups have come up to me at Top of the Pops and I've also had messages via the boys who played on it, for instance, who have been working with hairy groups – if you pardon the expression – and they've said 'Miss You Nights' is fantastic. Which is a great boost

RECORDING IN SPAIN/DEZO HOFFMAN, REX FEATURES

for my ego and gives me more incentive to get involved. (1976)

'Devil Woman'

The lyrics aren't risqué. I mean they're self-explanatory really, it's crystal balls.

When first we recorded it, I was a little worried about one line in the lyric that said "And I knew just what I came here for," so I altered it to "I wondered what I came here for."

Actually the lyric is anti-spiritualist. It's a warning. Beware. I'm not trying to preach at anyone, but it's a very dangerous area; black magic, spiritualists, mediums, etc.

I was talking to a minister in Birmingham who told me that black magic not only affects people mentally, but physically. He'd seen people who, because they'd dabbled in it, ended up with broken arms and legs.

When I read up on it in the Bible it emphatically says don't do it – and if God says it's dangerous, then it must be. (1976)

I believe the Bible tells us we shouldn't dabble with spirits that chirp and mutter, and 'Devil Woman' is very definitely against this kind of mystical experience.

I don't *have* to give a message every time I sing a rock'n'roll song, but if I get the

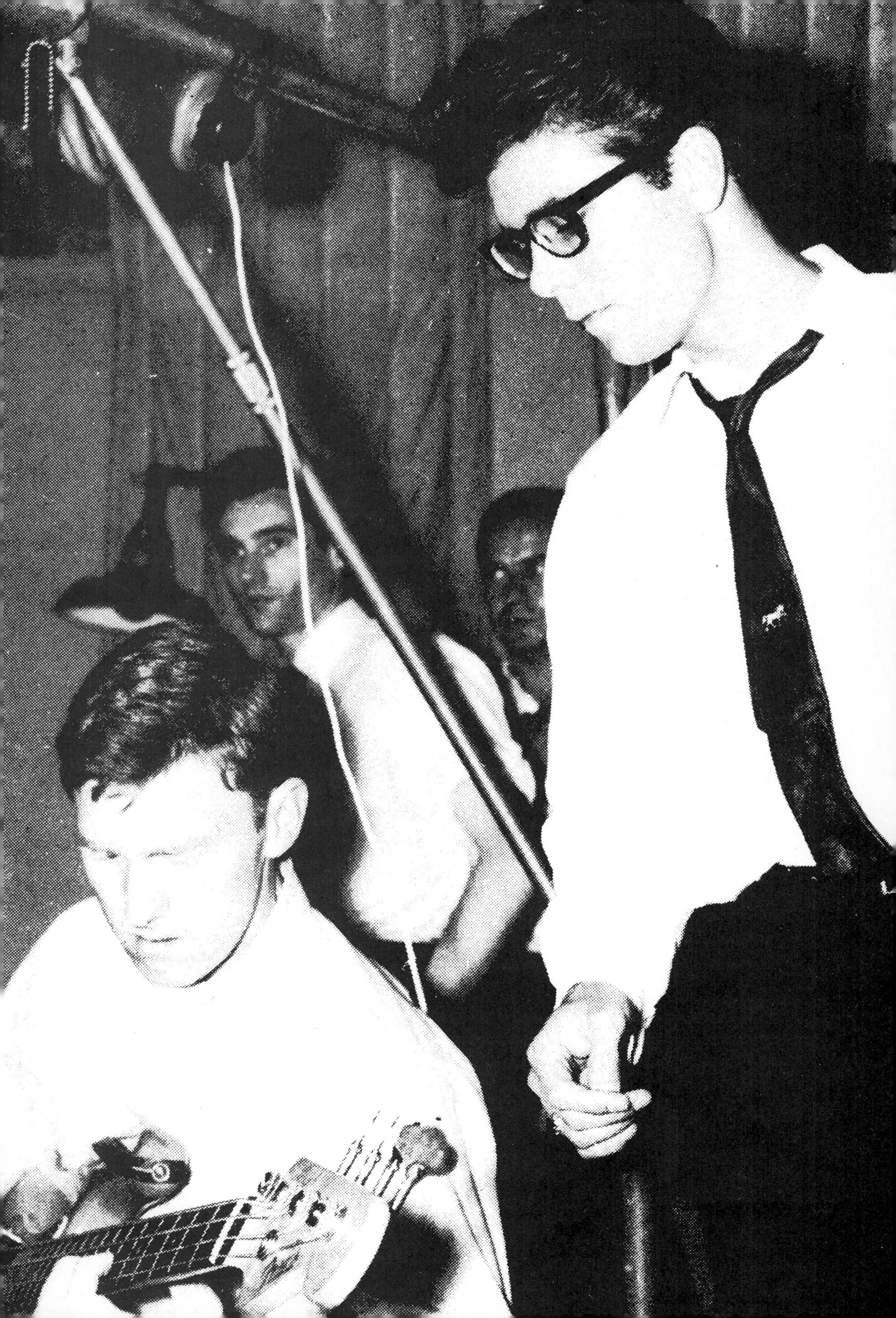

chance I should've thought Christians would've backed me all the way. I mean, I get enough criticism from the normal, non-Christian world without having to deal with it from within The Family.

I don't think there's any form of music that wasn't created by God, and so, to me, it's marvellous that I can sing rock'n'roll for Him, as opposed to singing it for the other bloke. (1976)

'I'm Nearly Famous.'

I had these two songs, 'Devil Woman' and 'I Wish You'd Change Your Mind And Stay,' and Bruce Welch also had four or five written by Allison & Sills. We also heard another forty songs and choose the best of the bunch. Then we went into the studios to begin work on the album.

It took us about a month in all, but that wasn't working every day; sometimes we'd go in at two and finish at five-thirty, or we'd record in the evenings from seven till ten, and obviously we'd work a lot of overtime. I reckon that if you put the session altogether, it was done in a fortnight.

A lot of today's artists take longer because they write the material in the studio. I mean I couldn't ever do that. I'm too impatient. Besides I know just what

I want – I've been doing it for long enough, practice makes perfect.

I love working in a studio, to me the studio is therapy, it's very relaxing, no stress. (1976)

There really has been the most amazing buzz about this album, and it started as long ago as while we were actually recording.

A couple of the guys working on the sessions actually came up and asked if they could have a copy of the album when it was finished! That's unheard of, normally they wouldn't give me a second thought. (1976)

When we first gave the finished tapes to the record company, they went wild. I was amazed. I thought, "You mean they actually like it?" When it came out, I wondered if the press would do the same old knocking bit, but they actually liked it too. I was bowled over!

Bruce knows what I can and can't do. I mean, I can't sing like Robert Plant, so I don't even try to! But I can do a rocky number like 'Devil Woman' and I can do a soft ballad like 'Miss You Nights.' Those I think are the two extremes of any sort of music.

Bruce and I knew we could do an album like 'I'm Nearly Famous' – it was just a matter of finding the right material. You see, the trouble was that when people knew the songs were for me, they kept coming up with stuff that sounded like 'Congratulations.'

So this time, Bruce didn't tell anyone who the songs were for. He knew what he wanted and he went out looking for it. And what he came up with were the sort of good rocking numbers I sang right back at the beginning of my career.

It's a big surprise, because I've known for a long time that some people just can't take me. They don't understand what I believe, they reckon I'm too good, too wholesome…

Not that I mind having that sort of image. I'm happy to have people think that about me. Even if they are wrong! I talk too much for a start. I'm fairly free and easy and I'm too truthful. It's always getting me into trouble.

'Small Corners.'

I wanted to prove that pop songs with words about God don't have to be anything like people's pre-conceived ideas of Gospel music.

But I'm not trying to convert anyone to Christianity. You can't judge what effect you are having by counting heads.

A lot of people still don't think it's "cool" to like me, and I keep seeing record reviewers almost apologising for liking my album.

But I don't think I have to justify singing about my views. No one else does, and that includes people such as Kris Kristofferson, Seals & Croft and even Elvis Presley. (1978)

The title of my new album 'Small Corners' was conceived from the old children's hymn which ends with the line, "You in your small corner and I in mine." I thought as I was doing my own thing in my small corner it was an apt title. I really feel this one is a part of me! In twenty years it's the only album of my own that I've produced.

'We Don't Talk Anymore.'

Bruce Welch is my producer and I trust his judgement. He has a great feel about a good song. I think there's some great bass and drums on this record. Maybe, of course, that's why it's making an impact in discos, for those two ingredients are important for the sound in disco evenings.

I can't say though that the record is disco. Let me say this as well. I like disco, but I can never tell the difference with bass and drums pre-eminent. We have these two things but the song comes first.

I mean it tells you what it's about, love breaking down. I notice the ad the company has been taking out – "They're not talking about it, they're playing it" – it gives another shade of meaning. (1979)

NG ONES
Cliff Sings
KOSTBARKEITEN
When Spain...
SCHALLPLATTEN
RICHARD and THE SHADOWS
CLIFF'S
LANG-SPIEL-PLATTEN
DM 18.-

CLIFF RICHAR
IN NEW YORK !

Cliff's Travels.

America.

'Living Doll' made the US charts during his first tour there...

It's bad machinery. We were there. We thought we really had it sewn up. We went on tour with "The Biggest Show Of Stars From 1960" and we weren't even on the bill, but "Added Attraction From Great Britain" was "Cliff Richard & The Drifters."

We went onstage and that first night we stopped the show. And there was Freddie Cannon, Bobby Rydell, The Clovers, The Crests, Clyde McPhatter.

That first night we got on to the coach to drive to the next place – overnight trip it was. Tough at the top in those days (laughs). Anyway, we got on the coach and the roadie said (American accent), "Well, guys, I think we Americans have got to give a round..." and they all applauded. I thought, "This is fantastic."

Every night we stopped the show. (1976)

In 1962 I came over to do something with a movie during the Cuban missile crisis. Nobody showed up. I was virtually overlooked. As far as the United States is concerned, everything has gone wrong.

When I'm ready to play the States on my own, it's got to work. I plan to bow out gracefully. After all, I've been with six different labels. (1976)

Cliff toured America to promote 'I'm Nearly Famous' in August 1976…
If I don't crack America with them I'm not going to bother anymore. It just means that they don't like me and that's it. I'm prepared to accept that. (1976)

The visit did me a lot of good. I've had a Top Five hit over there with 'Devil Woman.' I did a lot of radio stations and was knocked out that some of the black stations were playing 'Can't Ask For Anything More Than You' which has been released as a single. (1976)

Russia.

My manager, Peter Gormley, phoned me about six months ago to say that the Russians were interested in a visit by me.

There's been a lot of talking about details, but it now seems everything has been ninety-five percent worked out.

Plans are for me to go there first in March to record an album. I'll take my band and add their string players. I'll sing Russian melodies with English words.

I shall then go back to Russia in August to do concerts in Moscow, Leningrad and possibly one other city. Meantime, the album will have been released there.

I've performed behind the Iron Curtain before, of course. In the early sixties I was the first British pop performer to do so when I visited Poland. I've also played in Yugoslavia and Rumania.

Naturally, I'm thrilled about going to Russia. I shall, of course, feature songs from the album in my shows. My act will include Gospel numbers as it usually does. I shall also go to church in Moscow and Leningrad.

If Christians are having hard times in Russia the least you can do is show solidarity with them. (1975)

GOS agency, which does all the light entertainment in Russia, asked me to come over. I believe Russia is having what

DEZO HOFFMAN

38
Stockh

they call a Cultural Exchange Time, and obviously because I was safely middle-of-the-road and wasn't going to throw things out of the window, they choose me.

I was quite a safe bet, I'm not that outrageous, although I personally knew whatever I did would be outrageous compared to what audiences there are used to.

But having been, I think it will be some time before any decadently provocative groups get there. Groups like that have no hope. You see, with the culture that theirs is and the régime they have, they're extremely concerned about the behaviour of their young people.

And consequently, the chances of the Stones being invited are nil, as theirs is a very sexual act and no one tries to pretend that it's not. The Russians wouldn't welcome it because it would be considered the worst of our Western Movement. (1976)

Amazing reception. I think that it certainly proved that rock'n'roll is the international language.

We played a normal two-hour set, and by the end they were all up on their feet clapping and stamping and they'd rushed to the front of the stalls.

The stage was invaded, and I got a couple of bear hugs from enormous bearded Russians. It was a fantastic reception. (1976)

Bangladesh.

Quite honestly I don't think I've ever seen so many horrific sights. I'll tell you something about my first couple of days.

We were invited to go to one of the Bahari camps where there were nurses sponsored by the TEAR fund working on a feeding programme. Mothers with starving and diseased babies are brought to them. There are so many and there is such a limit on food and help that decisions have to be made about which children have a chance of survival.

We arrived there about eight-thirty in the morning and after I'd been there for what seemed an age and was feeling utterly shaken by it all I said to someone with me that it must be time for lunch. She said it was only half-past ten! Those two hours were like a life-time.

I thought about the people who work there, often young girls. They must go through some shattering experiences and get terribly depressed.

I'll tell you a shattering story. One of the nurses asked me to guess the age of one baby. I thought there must be some kind of catch otherwise I suppose she wouldn't have put it the way she did. So I said it must be two weeks old. She then made the alarming statement of the child being 5½lbs in weight and its age, a year and a half! It died the next day.

There were countless children in a dreadful state and yet somehow many of them seemed to smile through it all. I don't think though, that I shall ever forget that 5½lb baby.

In the kind of situation you find out there it almost seems as if humanity stops being human. People are fighting for survival and have no time for love. A mother has to choose between babies and there comes the point when she has to say, "I cannot feed you, child." (1973)

I saw the horror of a lifetime within a few hours. When I first got back from Bangladesh I was terribly upset with the horror of what I'd seen.

My first idea was to give up my career, sell everything I owned, wear sackcloth and ashes and become a missionary. But is that the total answer? I realise that being rich is obviously not a bad thing, because I have seen the good that money can do.

I thought I knew all about poverty before I went. In fact, I had considered I was from a poverty-stricken family.

But compared with the guy dying there in Bangladesh, we were well off. Everyone in this country is a millionaire compared with the tragic people there. (1974)

One of the most terrible sights I saw was a baby eighteen months old, who weighed

WITH TAY, A VIETNAMESE REFUGEE ADOPTED BY FRIENDS

only 5½lb. Many babies here weigh more than that when they are born. It died shortly after I saw it and must have been dying as I watched it.

I also saw the end of an operation on a little girl with a bullet lodged in her spine. They tried to hand the little bloodied bullet to me. But I'm afraid I chickened out. The girl was alive – just – but she's now paralysed for life from the waist down. (1974)

I walked through refugee camps and found the conditions horrifying.

I saw nurses having to make life or death decisions on whether or not they could help a sick child. They have so little food and medical supplies that they can only ration help to those who have any sort of chance of survival. It's a terrifying thing they have to do every day.

I showed myself up and suddenly realised that I wasn't very nice. We all talk about love, but it is so difficult to put it into practice. (1974)

It was really by accident that I first touched one of these children, all covered in sores. It was at a clinic and a group of them were being washed. They were sitting on a coconut mat all limp and drained of everything.

AT T.E.A.R. REFUGEE CAMP IN BANGLADESH

Then somebody accidentally trod on the finger of a little boy aged about three, who was sitting naked by my right elbow. He just screamed out like any kid would.

It was so natural. I've got a niece and nephew and I'm used to humping kids around and the next thing I just grabbed the little boy and he stopped crying instantly and just buried himself in my shoulder.

It was fantastic. I felt such a feeling of warmth, and forgot about the fact he was all sore-ridden. He was a little piece of humanity clinging to me. He stopped crying because all he wanted was a bit of affection and love.

The incident made such a deep impression on me that I have a blown-up

picture of me and the lad on the wall here in my home. No one sees it except me, because it's on the way to the loo. Every time I go by it reminds me of that situation out there. (1974)

At the airport there was a big car waiting to take me home to my lovely place here and everything seemed so unreal.

It seemed ridiculous that I should enjoy all this and that just over there, a matter of nine hours away, was that! It just didn't make sense.

I haven't got over it yet. And I don't want to get over it. It's a constant reminder to me of what is going on in other parts of the world. (1974)

Afterwords.

REX FEATURES

I mean people think I'm way past it. My only message to them is rock'n'roll transcends age. If you can sing it then you should be allowed to sing it. And if you happen to make a record which sounds nice and you happen to be sixty, well . . . and if you listen you shouldn't be put off by the person's age, it's the sound.

There was a time several years ago, when I almost lost interest because I was stuck in such an incredible middle-of-the-road bag. I did it at the time because it sold records, even though I disliked them. I've always been honest about it – I'm in the business to sell records.

But rock'n'roll is what it's all about. It keeps you young. If you have some affinity with it, you should be able to do it forever – as long as you have the energy. (1979)

However much I may hope to develop, I'm still very much a rock'n'roll singer at heart!